YOU CAN
HIT THE
GOLF BALL
FARTHER

YOU CAN HIT THE GOLF BALL FARTHER

by EVAN "BIG CAT" WILLIAMS
with Larry Sheehan

A Golf Digest Book

PHOTO CREDITS
All photos by Jack Mecca,
except page 13, Al Panzera;
pages 17 and 22, Bill Knight;
pages 25, 45, 121 and 126,
Anthony Roberts.

Published by Golf Digest, Inc.
A New York Times Company
495 Westport Avenue
Norwalk, Connecticut 06856

Trade Book distribution by
Simon and Schuster
A Division of Gulf & Western
    Corporation
New York, New York 10020

First Printing
ISBN: 0-914178-26-1
ISBN: 0-914178-29-6 (pb)
Library of Congress: 79-50544
Manufactured in the
    United States of America

DEDICATION

To my parents, to Champ Goldman for his guidance over the years, and to Dave Lamb and Babe Inganamort, who made me their regular caddie in the old days.

CONTENTS

ABOUT
BIG
CAT

1 about Big Cat

Big Cat, you routinely hit your tee shots well over 300 yards. Can other golfers learn to do that, too?

Maybe not quite that far, but from my observations in teaching and giving clinics and exhibitions, I would say that most golfers definitely could learn to drive the ball as much as 25 percent farther than they do presently.

How?

Through a concerted effort to adopt the right attitude and technique for handling the driver.

Is this what you propose to tell us?

I'd like to spell out the ingredients that have permitted me to hit a golf ball as far as I possibly can, and show how those ingredients can work for other golfers.

I'd like to get a quick picture of your big-hitting achievements first. What's the longest you've ever hit a golf ball?

Once I hit one 490 yards. It was in a pro-am, on the par-5 first hole at the Country Club of Siam, in Thailand. The hole is 570 yards long and we measured my drive by stepping off what yardage was left between the green and the ball. The fairways were hard and I got a lot of roll. But I wasn't feeling well at the time. I was on my first Far East tour, tired from the travel and sick from the food. I was surviving on fried rice and Coke. You don't have to feel strong as an ox to hit the ball far. In fact, it's better that you don't.

Were you playing the British ball that day?

No. That might have added 20 yards to the shot. The smaller British ball offers less wind resistance. The difference can be dramatic if you hit it long in the first place. For example, the exhibitions I've done at the Belmont Hotel Golf Course in Bermuda have been held on the first hole, which is only 305 yards long. Ten yards behind the green, there's a 20-foot-high stone wall. Beyond that is a street and on the other side of the street are houses. The first year down there I was driving into a strong wind, but managed to hit the wall on the fly. The second year the wind was behind me, so I carried the green with a 2-iron. Then I took out a driver and carried the wall. Then I teed up the British ball and knocked it against a chimney on one of the houses on the other side of the street.

How many long-driving shows do you put on these days?

I try not to schedule more than one or two clinics or exhibitions per week. If I have to hit a couple of hundred drivers over three or four days, my hands start to feel like hamburger.

Your way of hitting the ball, then, involves a lot of wear and tear?

No. I was talking about the few times when I've been overbooked and had to make an abnormal number of full shots in a short period. Actually, my longest drives don't feel hard at all because the blow of the clubhead on the ball is distributed throughout my body. That's what I try to get ordinary golfers to experience. Once they do feel that, they're on their way to longer drives. A smooth, swinging motion lets you hit the ball much farther than a jerky, muscular effort does.

Big Cat during one of his numerous exhibitions.

What's the biggest gallery you've had so far?

We had nearly 8,000 people show up in Tokyo one year. This particular exhibition was held at a driving range that was no bigger than a Datsun. I was bouncing irons off the back fence, but they kept saying, "Hit dwiver! Hit dwiver!" So finally I took out the driver and put a couple of shots into the traffic on the highway and nearly caused an accident.

When did you start getting famous for sending golf balls into orbit?

I got semi-famous beginning in July 1974. A comedian friend of mine named London Lee got me into a long drive contest held at Grossinger's, where he was performing. The resort had arranged a shoot-out between Jim Dent, one of the pro tour's longest hitters, and a couple of amateur sluggers, Jack DePalo from Westchester, and Dick Middleton from Hershey, Pa. London knew how far I hit the ball because we'd played golf together a lot, so he convinced the promoters to let me participate. At this time I was an assistant pro at Cedar Hills Country Club in Livingston, N.J., age 26, working with Bob Shields and his wife Gloria in the shop.

The rules were we each could hit a dozen balls, longest shot in the fairway to win. Dent hit first. He caught his sixth ball flush and it went 359 yards. Jim promptly sat down, saying that was the best shot he had in him instead of hitting the rest of the balls. And, in fact, that was about the longest drive I'd ever seen hit by another human.

I got up and on my fifth try put it out there past Jim's, at 366 yards. I kept hitting, though, because I was worried about the amateurs. But when their turns came, the best they could do was Middleton, 342, and DePalo, 331.

What did you win?

There wasn't any prize money, but I got lots of publicity. Joe DiMaggio happened to be in the crowd watching the contest, for example, and he told the press I was unreal and ought to be put in a cage, things like that. For months afterward I got clippings in the mail. Newspapers from all over the world had picked up the story. It was the first time in years any kind of effort had been made to establish who might be the biggest hitter in golf. It was different, fun, and it focused on an aspect of the game that all golfers could relate to.

Yet you didn't make a nickel out of it? Not directly, but it led almost immediately to my earning my first appearance money for hitting the ball long. Babe Lichardus was giving a clinic at Deal Country Club on the Jersey shore and, just for the hell of it, head pro Mike Burke hired me to come down anonymously and sit in the audience. Babe spoke about the golf swing for 20 minutes or so to the group gathered around the first tee, then picked me out as the "volunteer" who would attempt to apply some of the things he'd been talking about. The opening hole at Deal is only 310 yards long with a high hedge behind the green separating it from the street.

Babe teed up a ball for me, fussed around with my grip and stance for a bit and finally told me to see if I could make a decent pass at it. So I sailed it over the green, over the hedge and into the street. That stunned the group good.

It convinced them that Lichardus could teach? They swore by Babe's golf fundamentals from then on.

Outside of contests and exhibitions, what's been your longest clout with the U.S. ball in the United States? That would be 440 yards. I did it during a round with some club pro friends at Colony West Country Club in Fort Lauderdale. I just about carried the hole, the par-four 13th slight dogleg left. I hit the drive dead straight over a clump of 70-foot-tall trees at the corner and it reached the green on the second bounce. Normally, I have to play a full pitching wedge for my second shot on that hole.

Gee, that's tough. Anyway, I don't usually get excited about long drives, but this time I jumped up and down a few times. I missed the 15-foot putt for eagle because I was overly thrilled.

Have you ever aced a par 4? No. I've come close a lot of times. I've rattled flagsticks on the fly. Once I hit a 4-wood to within six inches on a 340-yarder. I've come close to a lot of double eagles on par 5's, too, but so far I haven't made one.

Do most people really believe how far you can hit the ball?

They're skeptical until they see me hit one, and then they go in the other direction. They tend to exaggerate, like fishermen. Once I hit a 5-iron to the middle of the green on the 238-yard eighth hole at Haworth (N.J.) Country Club. That's some kind of shot. But a couple of years later I went back and they were saying I flew the green with an 8-iron. Another time I was playing Bay Hill in Orlando. The sixth hole there is a long par 5 around a lake. Just for fun I tried to carry the lake with my tee shot. I would have had to drive it 360 or 370 yards on the fly to get it there. I was short by five yards and left it in the lily pads. But by the next time I got to Bay Hill, it was common knowledge that I had, in fact, reached the green.

So, some of my shots get longer every year without any work by me.

Are you regarded as a menace to society on some courses because of how hard you hit the ball?

People who don't know my game might take it for granted that I'm wild off the tee and so they think they've got to watch out. A couple of times guys have been hit by golf balls at the same time I was out on the course, and each time word got around that I was the perpetrator.

They've measured your ball to go as fast as 140 miles per hour, so if it did hit somebody, it might smart.

The only time I ever even came close was during a qualifying round for the New Jersey State Open held at Essex City Country Club. The 14th hole there is a 350-yard par 4, uphill all the way. I have a tendency to overhit on that hole because I'm always trying to reach the green with my drive. Anyway, this day I produced a vicious hook and it almost took out my No. 1 fan, a fireman who follows me around all the time when I'm in local tournaments. He was sitting on his portable stool off the fairway at about 260 yards when I teed off. I saw him hit the dust and thought for sure I'd gotten him, especially since my ball took a funny bounce and ended up back in the fairway instead of in the garbage where it belonged. But it turned out I had missed him. He's the last guy in the world I'd want to hit because I always score well when he's in the gallery.

The final standings at Pebble Beach in 1977.

national long driving championship

SPONSORED BY
BUICK
and E.F. HUTTON & CO.

NAME	DISTANCE
1 E. WILLIAMS	353^{24}
2 C. DUNN	346^{10}
3 A. SHEEN	326^{35}
4 S. ALTGELT	$322^{1/2}$
5 R. IREY	$319^{34 1/2}$
6 J. DENT	$316^{34 1/2}$

CONDUCTED BY
GOLF DIGEST, THE PGA OF AMERICA AND THE PGA TOUR

CHAMPIONSHIP FINALS
PEBBLE BEACH GOLF LINKS

Are you more wild off the tee than the average golfer? Less wild. You've got to realize that when I'm playing a round, even if it's only for a $2 Nassau, I'm driving for position more than for distance. For normal play I don't even use the club I take to long driving contests. I use what amounts to a 2-wood. I'm interested in scoring well, just as any golfer is. I might go for maximum distance on a certain hole, just for a stunt, or if the hole is so constructed that I won't be penalized if I do wander. I always say, blessed be the golf course architect who invented parallel fairways. Prodigious distance off the tee allows you to play from the wrong fairway a lot of times with no disadvantage, and sometimes with a decided edge.

Do you hit your irons as long, proportionately, as you do your woods? Yes. I hit the pitching wedge 150-155 yards as a rule. I can hit a 7-iron over 200 yards if I'm striving for effect, 185 yards if I'm putting my normal swing on it. I've hit 2-irons that go 300 yards.

How does that compare with the touring pros? I'm about three clubs longer than most of the pros. The average touring pro hits the 7-iron, say, about 150 yards.

Some pros have said you're actually too long to play on the circuit? It's not so much that I'm too long but that the gaps between the distances I get with my irons are too big. I don't have as much precision on approach shots as I would need to get within good scoring range consistently. The typical touring pro has an 8- or 9-yard gap between consecutive irons, which allows him to pinpoint his approaches. I've got 15 yards. I hit my normal 7-iron 185, my normal 6-iron 200, and so on.

I don't see what's so bad about that! It means I've got to hit the same club different distances all the time to get near the pin, and that requires extra finesse, extra feel. On a 140-yard shot into a green, for example, I might have to hit a three-quarter pitching wedge, whereas another guy could hit a full 8-iron. It's easier to be successful putting your automatic full swing on it every time than it is to be constantly inventing shots to make the ball go the right distance.

Then there's no way you could play the tour?

I could try the tour but I'd have to change my game. I'd have to close the gaps in my irons either by making them weaker—increasing the clubface loft on each of them—or by developing a three-quarter swing or punch-type stroke as my standard iron swing. And I'd have to replace the graphite shaft in my present driver with a stiffer shaft to improve my control off the tee and bring my drives down to the 300-yard range.

But once I made all those changes, the entertainment value in my shotmaking would be gone. People really enjoy seeing me hit the ball out of sight and sharing in some of my adventures, and that's why I like what I'm doing.

It's unnerving to reflect on the distances you can get—150 yards with a wedge, 200 yards with a 7-iron, 300 yards with a 2-iron. How far can you hit the putter?

I'll tell you, seriously, I once hit a ball 240 yards with a mallet-type putter, just as a joke. I broke the head off the thing.

How many drivers have you broken?

Just two in the past 10 years, each time on a routine drive when the clubhead split. But unlike putters, drivers are built to take the punishment if you hit the ball squarely. Guys who break a lot of clubs just don't hit their shots on the screws.

Are women interested in your act?

There's a kind of "Me-Tarzan-you-Jane" aspect to the long drive department, but usually only if the woman involved truly understands the game. Once I was proceeding through Customs on my way back from an overseas trip when I noticed two attractive blondes in the line eyeing me pretty closely. One of them finally came up and patted my golf bag, which had on it in big letters: EVAN WILLIAMS - NATIONAL DRIVING CHAMPION. She smiled and said in an extremely friendly voice, "Are you really the national driving champ?"

I smiled back and admitted I was, and was all set to negotiate for her phone number, when she remarked, "Then you must know Mario Andretti!"

Do you get many betting propositions?

A couple of times guys have talked about going head to head off the tee with me for $5,000, but each time I put up the cash they'd disappear. The Fat Man (Marty Stanovich, a well-known professional gambler) wanted to fly me to Hawaii one time to trade shots with a guy out there for $25,000, but at the last minute his pigeon backed out.

Come to think of it, the only distance bet I ever really collected on was back in my caddying days at Englewood Golf Club, the former U.S. Open site that is now in ruins in my hometown of Leonia, N.J. I used to scout neighboring courses for an avid golfer named Dave Lamb. He liked to have local knowledge when he had to play a match away from Englewood, so he'd pay me to play the places in advance and gather intelligence on the greens.

On one such expedition, I happened to hit a 5-iron to the green on a 232-yard par-3 hole. This caused a stir among some witnesses and word got back to the clubhouse before I did. There was one Doubting Thomas among the members to greet me when I finished the round. Right away he said I couldn't possibly have reached the green on that par 3, not even with a 4-iron. I had my $20 bill from Dave Lamb in my wallet so I bet him I could. We went back out to the hole together and I airmailed the green with the 4, as I knew I would, and collected the guy's $20.

I felt kind of bad about that bet since it was a foregone conclusion I would win. But I ran into the same guy a year later and we became friends. I found out losing the $20 hadn't hurt him that much because he was a multimillionaire.

That's the extent of my earnings as a hustler.

Englewood had a reputation as a hot-bed of high rollers for a while, didn't it?

Englewood went through a lot of different phases before it gave up the ghost. Yeah, there were some Cosa Nostra types playing there for a while when I was a caddie. They were hard-hearted guys who made it a practice to look after No. 1 long before that book ever came out. One day I was caddying for some gamblers when we came to the 10th hole. There we got word that a guy in the foursome ahead of us had just died from a heart attack and his body was lying on the 11th green. The first gambler hears this and wants to quit playing the round out of respect for the dead. The second gambler disagrees and suggests that they merely skip the 11th hole and come back and play it later after the warm body has been removed. The third gambler disapproves of this because if the holes aren't played in order it will screw up the presses. Finally, the fourth gambler makes the decision:

"Let's just keep going the way we are."

"What about the guy lying on the green?" asks someone.

"Simple," the fourth gambler replies. "Play him as casual water."

Funny story if you like sick humor. Actually, those guys weren't typical of the membership at Englewood.

A jubilant Big Cat after winning his second National Long Driving title.

Dave Lamb was and is today, actually, the epitome of the competitive club golfer. He ran a very successful insurance agency back then, but his mind was usually on his golf matches. I remember once he called me at 3:30 in the morning, on the day of a match.

"Hello Evvie! Dave Lamb here!"

"What's the matter?" I'm genuinely concerned, because Dave's always been good to me. He'd never fail to send a waiter from the clubhouse out to the caddie pen with an egg sandwich for me, just so he was sure I'd had a good breakfast before carrying his bag for him.

"I'm down at the office," he says.

"But what's so urgent? It's 3:30!"

"Listen, Evvie, I've been thinking. On 18, do you think we ought to stick with the wedge, or go back to the 9-iron formula?"

Now I see the light. Dave is concerned about the match he's got scheduled for the day, and specifically about the approach shot on the finishing hole—when all the presses will be riding.

"You woke me up to ask that?" I say.

"Evvie, don't fool around with me, this is important. We got Bernie in a few hours."

Then I made the mistake to humor him. "All right, why don't we try the 9-iron into the green instead of the wedge for a change?"

"In that case, Evvie, we got to get out to the course much earlier to try out 100 balls using the 9-iron formula."

So I had to get up an hour sooner.

Who was Bernie?   Bernie Leentil was Dave Lamb's nemesis on the links. They were an interesting contrast. Dave was short and balding, wore glasses and didn't look real athletic. Bernie was the Robert Wagner type— well-built, blond, handsome, popular with men, women and caddies. Dave played an intense plug- ger's game, short off the tee and deadly on the greens. Bernie had a more flamboyant style. He could birdie more holes than Dave could, but he could get into more trouble, too, especially when he started hooking it.

Anyway, Dave and Bernie regularly bet it up. I remember another time I staggered in from a heavy date in the city at around 4 a.m. only to find a note saying, "DAVE WILL PICK YOU UP AT 5:45 A.M." I immediately woke up my mother and told her there was no way I could caddie for anybody in my condition. So she agreed that when Dave showed up she would tell him I hadn't ever returned from New York. Forgetting about Dave Lamb's persistent nature, I went to bed. A cou- ple of hours later I hear Dave honking the horn on his Lincoln Continental. I roll over. A few minutes later I hear stones against my bedroom window. I roll over again. I'm half awake and bleary-eyed. All of a sudden I see something at the window, which is on the second story. Dave Lamb has climbed straight up at least 20 feet to press his face against the windowpane and holler, "Evvie, what are you doing in bed? We got Bernie this morning!"

Enjoying the taste
of victory.

When did it dawn on you that there was something uncommon about your golf game?

I began driving the ball more than 300 yards when I was 15. I lived right behind the 12th green at Englewood and in the evenings, after caddying all day, I'd go out with a couple of pals and we'd play until the man on the tractor ran us off. We'd get onto other good private courses in the area by the ploy of dating the daughters of greenkeepers, no matter what they looked like. Anyway, I regularly put it past the other guys, who were pretty long hitters themselves. I didn't pay much attention to it, though, mainly because my energies as an athlete were mostly directed into basketball.

A fellow named Chiefie was the closest thing we had to an intellectual in my group growing up. Chiefie dressed like a Yalie long before he had ever heard of the Ivy League. He would not be seen in public without his Madras pants and penny loafers. Anyway, he was the guy who put into perspective the activities of everyone else in the group, and about my long hitting he said if I wasn't careful I would grow up to be a living legend. But as I say, my mind was on basketball.

Was there anything special about your golf swing?

I wasn't really aware of what I was doing, except that I know two things were there naturally from the start—a big shoulder turn on the backswing and really good lateral movement on the downswing. I was built like a bean pole at this time—5 feet 7 inches tall and only 110 pounds. My heroes were Tony Lema, Chi Chi Rodriguez and Arnold Palmer. I remember reading somewhere during this period that Palmer's father had encouraged Arnie as a youngster to hit the ball hard and not to worry about keeping it straight until later. This turned my own inclinations to swing all out into Gospel Truth.

Do you think it's possible to understand human nature if you've never been a caddie?

I doubt it. They should make all psychiatrists carry bags of clubs and see life through a caddie's eye for one summer, instead of reading Freud.

When did your own caddying days end?

I can't remember the last time I actually carried for a round, but I do know the exact time I realized that phase of my life was behind me. I was sitting in the caddie pen at Englewood, playing blackjack, when a guy comes out from the club and announces there's a phone call for me from Red Holzman, who, it turns out, wants to invite me to the New York Knicks try-out camp later that summer. The other caddies gape at me. They know I've compiled a good record as a college basketball player, but still it is jarring to them to suddenly imagine that one of their own kind might join the likes of Willis Reed, DeBusschere, Frazier, Bradley and the rest—the Knicks are in their championship years right now.

So this phone call alters how my fellow caddies see me, which from now on is a little bit sideways. And as for what's changed in me, it has to do with the fact that I turn down Red Holzman's invitation. Honestly, I don't think I'm good enough to make it as a Knick at this time, but beyond that, in my own mind, I've dropped my first love, basketball, for golf. In fact, I've already put my name in for an assistant pro's job right there at Englewood. I don't get that job until fall, so for the rest of the summer I continue to caddie. But from about the day of that phone call, the way I looked at myself and at golf was totally different.

BIG CAT'S KEYS TO EXTRA YARDAGE OFF THE TEE

reaching your true potential off the tee

Realistically, what is the average weekend golfer's chances for adding more distance?

High-handicappers who slice the ball now could add 25-50 yards to their tee shots, depending on how much they cut the ball in the first place. Most men of average skill and fitness ought to be able to hit the ball 230, at least, if they use the right technique and mental approach. Most women golfers, who presently hit it out there 150-175, I'd say, should be able to reach 200.

Do most golfers have a clear idea of how far they're hitting the ball?

Not even touring pros drive the ball as far as most people think they do. A few years ago IBM surveyed a number of PGA tournaments and computed that the average length of a drive on tour was 264 yards.

I've never heard a male golfer admit to a drive of less than 200 yards. Usually they're claiming 230, 240, 250 and up.

Not all, but most—I'd say 80 percent—of the men exaggerate the length they're getting on all their clubs, and especially with their drivers which, after all, is the ultimate macho instrument in the game.

Exaggerate by how much?

By 25-50 yards, in many cases. I've played with guys who tell me they've hit the ball 270 yards a few times, but who have golf swings that make it physically impossible for them to reach anything like that distance, unless there are hurricane winds behind them on the tee.

Is it that simple—you look at a person's swing and know how far he can hit the ball?

If you have no weight shift, you lose yards. If you hit from the top, you lose yards. If you have no hand release as the clubhead comes into the ball, you lose yards. If you have no finish, you lose yards. All these things are easy enough to see and then you know right away you're dealing with a guy who hits singles, not home runs.

Singles to right field?

Slicers, yes.

What's so bad about the slice if it stays in the fairway?

Nothing, if you're not interested in getting maximum distance. If you are, then the slice is holding you back. The draw swing pattern generates greater distance because the club comes from inside the line and the hands release fully at the correct time. This allows the ball to fly on a lower, more penetrating trajectory than it does when it's sliced. The greater amount of backspin on the sliced shot, due to the fact that it is hit with an open clubface, also causes the sliced drive to "check" more when it does land. If you carry a drive 200 yards, it will roll maybe 10 yards if it's got left-to-right slice spin on it. But it may roll 25 yards if it's a right-to-left spinning draw or hook. When they call a guy "sneaky long" that's what they mean—his ball rolls a long time after it hits.

What's the difference between a hook and a draw?

A hook moves quickly and uncontrollably from right to left. If you start a shot out along the right side of the fairway and it travels all the way over to the left side of the fairway before it lands, you've hit a hook.

A draw moves from right to left in a controlled manner. If you start a shot out along the right side and it finishes in the middle of the fairway, that's a draw.

The draw is what we're after?

It has the extra distance of the hook without the problem of wildness.

So as a slicer, my first goal should be to start to draw the ball?

Your first goal should be to develop a full swinging motion and the proper hand release, as we'll explain shortly, and not to worry at all about your flight pattern or where the ball is going. Build the swing before you start analyzing the shot.

What should I do if I start hooking?

If you've been a slicer, you should jump in the air for joy, because it means you've altered your swing dramatically. Your past history as a slicer will make it easy to work back in the other direction to bring the hook under control and transform it into a draw.

But don't a lot of the touring pros hit the fade, which is a controlled slice, and not the draw?

Sure, but they're out there 250 yards to start with, because they've got tremendously well-developed golfing muscles. They don't need extra yards the way the weekend golfer does.

I suppose it's human nature to inflate one's distances?

Sure, but it's also easy simply to be misled about yardage. Many driving-range operators aren't too fussy about where they set down the distance markers, for example. You can make your customers feel like King Kong off the rubber mats if you set the 250-yard marker in at 220. Or take a situation out on the golf course. Suppose you reach the 150-yard bush on your tee shot on a 410-yard dogleg? That means you've driven the ball 260, right? Well, not necessarily. You may have cut 15-20 yards out of the hole by driving the ball off the tee at an angle. And the bush itself may be 160 yards from the center of the green instead of 150. That would mean you've actually driven it 230, not 260.

I've always trusted those 150-yard bushes!

Most are accurate to within a few yards, but you'll find some that are off by quite a bit. The guy who stepped off the location might have been a giant, with a $3\frac{1}{4}$-foot stride, or he might have been dragging so bad at the end of a long, hot day that he only had a $2\frac{3}{4}$-foot stride. Either way, he counts 150 strides, plants the bush, waters it good, and the net distortion amounts to 17 yards.

Big Cat sets his feet in a slightly open stance (frames 1-2), but strives to keep his shoulders square. By hip height (frame 4), his wrists are almost completely set. While his left wrist is square at the top (frame 7), weaker

players may have to cup their wrists slightly here. Note that the club is not overswung past parallel.

Legs lead the downswing (frame 9). At impact (frame 12), weight is almost entirely on the left side. Big Cat's excellent extension shows in frame 13 as

the clubhead "chases" the ball. In a proper full-finish position (frame 16), the hands are higher than the head.

That measurement is taken from the center of the green?

That's right, so if you hit a 5-iron from the bush to the front of the green, it doesn't mean you've hit the 5-iron 150 yards as you might have thought. There could be another 10-15 yards to the center of the green and you'd have to take that into account in determining exactly how far you'd hit your 5-iron.

How accurate are yardages printed on scorecards?

If the course has been set by the USGA or by one of the regional golf associations, they should be accurate. Even so, remember that tee markers are moved every few days by the greenkeeper to spread the wear and tear of traffic all throughout the teeing area. There's usually some kind of permanent marker on the tee that relates to the exact yardage shown on the scorecard. But the tee markers themselves could be set 5 to 15 yards in front of or in back of that spot on the day you play.

A lot of people say they can't handle the driver. They go with a 3-wood off the tee.

There are times when you'd want to use a fairway wood or an iron off the tee. But you'd be foolish to regularly deprive yourself of the extra distance a driver can give you. Also, it's more fun to hit than any other club. Playing golf without a driver is like watching TV in black and white.

People say the clubface is too straight for them.

It's got plenty of loft for the job. I can get more height with my driver off the tee than I do using a 3-wood off a perfect lie in the fairway. Teed up, the ball is a sitting duck for any reasonably good swing.

Is the driver swing much different from the iron swing?

The extra length on the shaft and the fact that the ball is suspended an inch or so off the ground allow you to launch the ball with more of a sweeping action of the clubhead. With an iron you strike down on the ball more sharply to get it airborne.

What does "launching the ball" feel like to you?

My upper body stays behind the ball a little more than it does on iron shots and the clubhead stays square to the target longer. I can feel that ball flatten out when I make a really good driver swing, as though it sticks to the club for an instant.

Are you promoting increased distance with just the driver, or with all the clubs?

The driver is the main club you should get all you can out of. With irons, people should be happy just to hit them consistently and with control. If you've been a slicer and get reborn as a hooker, chances are all your irons will get longer, too. But primarily you're going to try to go for maximum length on your drives and controlled length with your irons.

Is the payoff really worth the time and effort it would take to change the swing to get those extra yards?

The shorter you are off the tee right now, the more you stand to gain. If you can add 20 or 30 yards to your average tee shot, you will be playing a whole new ball game. But even a minimal increase in yardage could pay off. If you're a 5-handicap golfer and you find a way to add seven or eight yards to all your tee shots, you'll start to score two or three shots lower per round.

Why is that?

Because you'll be hitting one less club into the green, so you'll reach more greens in regulation.

In other words, if you can increase your distance off the tee, you'll be in a position to hit shorter and, therefore, more accurate irons into the greens.

The old way, you're always struggling to make 4 with a good chance to bogey. With longer drives, you're shooting for more birdies with a good chance to par.

What about on par 5's and par 3's?

You'll have a chance to reach more par 5's in two. Assuming your irons have gotten a little bit longer along with your wood clubs, you'll be hitting shorter irons into the par 3's and, once again, with the greater accuracy that comes with using shorter irons, you'll be looking at more makeable birdie putts.

Are there any other strictly tactical advantages of distance?

You'll be able to carry certain hazards or trouble spots, possibly, that you never could before. With the greater clubhead speed that is part and parcel of a power-producing swing, you'll be able to get out of rough more easily. You'll also be able to get more height on shots when you need it, like if you're blocked out by a tall tree.

What about psychological advantages?

Well, you're always feeling good about yourself as a golfer when you're booming your drives. It's like a perpetual ego massage. You're making the other guy feel like he ought to take up tennis after all. He may press his swing too hard and mis-hit a few, instead of playing his own game.

If you've got the longest drive, you're the last to hit the second shot on any given hole.

You get to see what everybody else is using into the green, which is bound to make your own club selection more accurate. You also get to see what effect any wind might be having on approach shots, and how the greens are holding.

I'm impressed by the various different benefits that long driving can offer. It makes it seem not only tempting, but logical to strive to master the driver, as you prescribe.

Yeah, it's a good idea to identify the specific ways that long driving can lead to lower scoring, because for a lot of people score is the bottom line, not showmanship off the tee, and that is what motivates them.

But golf is fun, too. Let's not forget the purely visceral kick people get out of hitting the ball far and straight without falling down. I've seen it in friends and pupils I've worked with, and I assure you that learning to nail all your tee shots consistently is in itself worth the price of admission.

Does your height of 6 feet 6 inches give you an extreme advantage in hitting the ball long?

The taller you are, the longer your swing arc can be, but that alone doesn't guarantee distance. There have been small players—guys under 5 feet 8 inches and weighing no more than 150 pounds—who've hit it over 300 yards in the long driving contests. Swing technique is more important than altitude.

Would you say your thoughts on technique are compatible with the way good club pros teach?

I've checked these things out with the host pros at a lot of the clubs where I've given clinics or exhibitions. We're in the same ball park. What I'm saying and showing about swing technique supports their own efforts on the lesson tee. At least that's what the pros themselves have told me.

You're not a gorilla with a one-of-a-kind new style for battering a golf ball. You're orthodox.

The distance I get is extraordinary, but my swing conforms to sound technical principles, and is actually representative of the most effective swings on the pro tour today. Nicklaus, Watson, Ballesteros, Lietzke, Bean, North and a few more of the players who have been winning most of the tournaments today, all hit the ball far. Their swings differ in numerous minor respects, but they are all alike in that they generate great power.

Is this the swing of the future?

I think eventually all the big money winners on tour will be long hitters, using basically the same technique these players use, and playing the game primarily with driver, wedge and putter.

Where do we go from here?

I'd like to explain my swing the way I would describe it to a group of golfers at a clinic, only in more detail. I'll stress as I go along those factors that I think are instrumental in creating power and adding length to drives.

What are the ground rules? Do you expect people to do everything you say?

Everything may be worth trying, but not all at once. I don't want people to turn themselves into knots in an effort to incorporate the things I think are important to distance.

Like most people, I'm always a bit wary of instruction, I guess, because if I do go out on a golf course with a lot of swing advice on my mind, I have a bad day.

Yes, well, don't change a flat tire in the middle lane of the Interstate. If you're going to make any of the changes or improvements that I advocate, do so on the practice tee, not during a round. I met a fellow on the first tee once who didn't understand the danger of analysis at the wrong time. He drew on his glove, then launched into one of the most impressive speeches on the golf swing I'd ever heard. It was practically a dissertation. But when it was his turn to hit, he shanked the ball dead right into the swimming pool.

breathe, don't seethe— swing, don't hit

What are the main things on your mind in going for distance?

There are two cardinal rules to follow.

First, you've got to stay nice and relaxed. The minute you tighten up, a kind of rigor mortis develops in your golfing muscles and prevents them from acting in a fluid, power-producing manner. Above your waist you become tense. Below your waist you're static. Golf is like basketball in that you need supple, fast-responding muscles throughout the body to execute well. Nervousness or anxiety keeps that from happening.

Second, you've got to be swing conscious and not ball conscious. A lot of potentially good golf swings are ruined by the mental picture players form of putting the clubhead on the ball, instead of swinging the club smoothly from the top, through the ball and to a high finish position. Ball-consciousness inserts a kind of STOP sign into the swing, reducing the centrifugal force built up.

I'm surprised you place such a high priority on being relaxed. I would not have related that directly to gaining distance.

I didn't realize how important it was until a few years ago when I conducted an experiment. Prior to that I had always had a tendency to muscle the ball in the firm belief it was getting me extra yards. Anyway, I went out on the course by myself one day. I had a dozen balls, six of them No. 1's, six of them No. 2's. First I hit the No. 1's. I stayed as relaxed as I could. I wasn't trying to put it out there too far, but rather just making a good swing. Then I hit the 2's. I killed them. I mean I really tried to hit them hard, and I was convinced, by the way I was smashing them, that they were sailing way past the 1's. But then I went down the fairway to collect the balls and, sure enough, the hard-hit 2's were all 10-15 yards shorter than the smoothly hit 1's. I did this a number of times and always got the same results.

Nowadays I see the same thing occur if I go to play 18 holes after giving a long driving exhibition. In the exhibition, no matter what I tell myself, I'll tend to hit the driver a little harder than normal. Then I'll go out to play afterward and tee off a nice, relaxed swing and put the ball 10 yards farther than any of my exhibition drives.

Are you saying that if a golfer is swinging as hard as he can, he can be sure he is losing distance?

Absolutely. If you feel you've hit the ball good and hard, you've actually lost yardage. Your feelings are contradictory to what actually happens.

So there's a peculiar logic about the golf swing that people have to get used to.

Swing easy and the ball will go out of sight. Hit it hard and it won't leave your shadow.

Could you actually hurt yourself swinging too hard?

Sure. The proper swing is relatively easy on the body. But if you go after the ball just with your arms and shoulders, you could hurt your lower back. If you swing without a good weight transfer, you could hurt the Achilles tendon in the back foot.

Big Cat's lower-body drive is the most remarkable aspect of his downswing.

Why is it golfers want to hit the ball so hard in the first place?

Because of what I just said. They equate maximum effort with maximum distance, which sounds reasonable but isn't.

Also, a lot of men played baseball as kids and they instinctively want to use the golf club the way they learned to operate the baseball bat—with arms, hands and shoulders. You need muscles to hit a golf ball far, but if those upper-body muscles tighten up, you can't use them effectively.

The big hitter in golf uses tempo and leverage, not brute strength, to get the ball out there a long way. It's like kicking long punts in football, which I did as a sideline in college. I wasn't bad at it. My longest went 76 yards. Another punt that the opposition made a fair catch on was timed by my coach as being in the air for 7½ seconds. My point is, I recall now that I always tried to have the same relaxed feeling when the football was hiked to me, prior to a punt, as I do when I prepare to launch an extra-long tee shot today.

I would think, in long driving contests where everything rides on just a few big swings, it would be almost impossible to relax.

It's hard. It's the downfall of most of the contestants who get to the finals. Bear in mind that some of these fellows may never have played in front of a crowd bigger than would fit in a station wagon. Now they've got a gallery of 5,000, a bunch of TV cameras trained on them, and a man in a blazer announcing their names and home towns. Some of the better known touring pros might be there out of curiosity. One year I recognized Hale Irwin, Jerry Pate and Johnny Miller on the sidelines. Most of the long driving contestants are in awe of such players. Now in front of these guys and all the rest, they've got to get up there and drive the ball as far as they possibly can. They are solid tension from head to toe.

The first-tee jitters that a lot of club golfers feel would be similar to that situation on a much smaller scale. How do you beat the tension?

Most contests of any kind are won the night before they're held—in the preparation you've done beforehand. Some of the long driving contestants get so unnerved by the atmosphere that they invent a different swing or tempo for the occasion. Instead of going with what got them there in the first place, they produce a brand new swing. That's why you see so many duck hooks, or shots skied way right. You have to go into this sort of thing with exactly the same technique that has worked for you in the past, and with the attitude that it is going to keep on working for you.

How did you control your nerves during Long Drive III at Pebble Beach when you had only one ball left and needed to put it in the fairway past the 320-yard mark to win the contest? How did you manage to gather yourself and hit it 353?

Well, the preparation I had done for the contest had given me the confidence I could produce the longest drive, so I didn't feel any pressure to do something novel. I had a technique I knew I could count on, and I was intent on beating the other guy systematically with that technique.

I told myself to stay relaxed, take it back nice and slow, trust what I got. I took a few quick breaths. I find that taking a few short breaths sometimes is more relaxing than taking one deep breath. Anyway, the oxygen works wonders on the system in a situation like that. It opens a valve and lets the excess pressure escape.

I always trust what I have on my practice swing, but put a ball in front of me and I sometimes lose the faith.

That's ball consciousness. You're thinking about hitting the ball instead of swinging the club the way you did when you knocked off the dandelion.

Don't you have to think about the ball, though? It's staring you in the face.

I look at the ball, but I don't think of placing that clubhead on the ball. I think of the ball getting in the way of the clubhead when I make a good swing.

Do you look at the top of the ball?

If I looked at the top of the ball, I would top it when I swung. I look at the back of the ball. That's where I want the clubhead to sweep through.

Is it true that even in good swings, the clubhead slows down somewhat prior to impact?

No, in a good swing the speed of the clubhead keeps increasing throughout the downswing. As it nears the ball, however, the speed is increasing at a slower rate.

Do poor players tend to "flinch" when they swing?

I think even the pros flinch a tiny bit as the clubhead gets near that ball. But the better your swinging motion, the more such anticipation of the hit is reduced and the more clubhead speed is conserved. Ideally, you swing through the ball the way a karate expert strikes with his hand, to a point somewhere beyond the piece of wood or brick he plans to demolish.

The ball is positioned opposite the left heel for the driver swing (frame 1). Big Cat sets the clubface slightly open at address to foster an inside-the-line takeaway. The left heel comes up to maximize turn on the backswing

(frame 4). At the top (frame 6), Big Cat is fully coiled, with weight braced on the inside of his back foot. He uses tremendous leg drive to initiate the downswing (frame 7).

Late release of wrists (frame 11) conserves clubhead speed. Notice in frame 13 how the left side is completely in control at impact. As you'll see

in Chapter 3, the strong grip not only encourages a high finish (frame 15), but also creates a burst of clubhead speed at the bottom that gets distance.

You can't even start to be swing concious unless you're relaxed. Is that true?

If you're not relaxed, your muscles aren't going to be able to take the club back smoothly to a good position at the top, then, in conjunction with a nice weight transfer and swing the club through to a high finish position. If you're ball conscious, you're more likely to be tense, and to hit *at* the ball rather than swing *through* it. Not long ago, pro George Knudson took part in a stress-measurement experiment by playing an entire round with his eyes closed. He shot 67 and according to the readings they took on him, his stress was lower with his eyes closed than when he played with his eyes open. The point might be, you have to have your attention on the ball to hit it, but it's better not to see it in great detail, because that type of obsessive concentration could hurt the swing.

Why do people get ball conscious?

It may come about when you first start playing the game. At that point you might be telling yourself that the one thing you want to avoid more than anything else in the world is to whiff the ball. So you inhibit your swinging motion in the interest of making contact and saving face.

Also, I think golfers carry around a mental picture of the ideal position at impact of club and ball, because it's been reproduced thousands of times in books and magazines and ads. You also get it right there in living color when you address your own ball. That's how things should look at impact, right? So if you're too much of a thinker, that's what you'll dwell on in the course of swinging, instead of concentrating on making the good fluid swing itself.

But you have to meet the ball squarely, right?

It's much more important to develop a swinging motion before trying to achieve solid or square contact. The swinging motion generates the clubhead speed that will give you good distance. If your main concern at the outset is to meet the ball right in the middle of the clubface, you'll automatically restrict your swing. You'll be putting the club on the ball, like a bunter in baseball, and your shots will go about as far as a bunt.

But when can you expect to start hitting them solid?

It depends on how good your natural hand-eye coordination happens to be, and how much time you devote, and I mean devote, to practicing the swinging motion. At first the novice hits the ball every which way. He's got to ignore those mis-hits, caroms and low bounders and concentrate on building the swinging motion. Gradually his intuitive hand-eye coordination will adjust and adapt and develop within him the specific reflexes he needs for golf, and at this time he'll begin to hit more balls squarely.

What if he doesn't ignore those mis-hits?

If he gets upset by them and decides he doesn't want to spray his shots around any more, he'll start thinking of putting the club on the ball instead of swinging the club. At first it may look like he's getting somewhere, because he probably will hit more shots straight. But he won't be generating as much clubhead speed that way, so the shots won't travel as far. In time this woeful lack of distance will begin to gnaw at him, so he'll tap his reserves of brute force and become a slasher. Now he's not only short, he's back to spraying his shots again.

How do you tell if you have a good swinging motion?

If your knuckles are white and your forearms are bulging with the exertion, you're probably not a swinger. Or look at the position of your club at the finish of your swing. If the club is pointing at the target or at the sky, it means you've hit at the ball. If your club is pointing behind you, it means you've made a good swing.

How does the player with an established hit-at-the-ball pattern build a good swing motion?

He's got to work at it on the practice range, conceding a large number of mis-hits, before he makes the transition from slash to swing. He may have to take one step backward before he can go two steps forward. It's a question of gradually developing the confidence and trust in the new swinging motion.

Aren't there any specific aids to developing better swing conscious-ness?

If you think "tempo," you'll get there faster. Swinging in rhythm stems from the ability to stay relaxed, too. Be patient and easygoing rather than quick and anxious in your approach to each shot. Where the ball goes doesn't count for now. How you swing the club is all that matters.

You should waggle the club a lot. Good veteran players may not waggle much only because their swinging motions are fully grooved. But if you're just building or rebuilding, the extra waggles will reinforce the feelings and the tempo in a good swing.

Checklist

Okay, I've got two concepts firmly implanted in my mind:

1. If I want to get all I can out of my driver, the first thing I've got to learn to do is stay relaxed. If I swing easy I'll hit it farther than if I try to kill the ball. I especially have to forget my days in the Little League and guard against any muscular tension in my upper body. I can't let my legs freeze on me. Keep breathing that good oxygen, stay limber, and let my golfing muscles do the job they know how to do.

2. I've got to cultivate a swinging motion that finishes with my club pointing directly behind me instead of up at the sky. I've got to watch the ball but not become obsessed with it. I want the ball to get in the way of the clubhead when I make the swing. I want to erase the idea of planting the clubhead on the ball, because ball consciousness is going to slow up my clubhead and cut down on my yardage.

3 the power-producing setup

Setting up to the ball correctly sets the stage for swinging for maximum distance.

The average golfer may not be able to successfully imitate my setup in every detail, but I think if he or she understands the principles I'm working with, and applies them in his own way to his own setup, he'll begin to see an improvement in the distance he's getting.

In a nutshell, the principles are these:

I'm adopting the *grip* that is going to make it possible for my hands to release fully into the shot when I do swing, without any conscious effort on my part.

I'm taking a *stance* in relation to the ball that will permit me to draw the shot—produce the right-to-left flight pattern of a draw rather than the left-to-right pattern of the slice.

I'm assuming a *posture* that will enable me to get maximum use out of all my golfing muscles. I'm going to make an athletic swing rather than a mechanical swing.

What's an athletic swing? In an athletic swing, you're using what you have instead of fighting what you have. Tom Weiskopf, Johnny Miller, Jerry Pate and Chi Chi Rodriguez are good examples of golfers with athletic rather than mechanical, by-the-numbers swings. A fringe benefit of the athletic swing is that you can play more creative shots with it. The swing is so closely linked to your individual nerves and musculature that you can make it react to special situations on the course better. Mechanical swings provide less flexibility.

Exactly how does the grip help or hinder the job of getting extra distance? The way you hold the club at address affects what you can or can't do with the club at impact. Kids with good athletic instincts will pick up a golf club and automatically assume what is called a "strong" grip, because they sense it is going to allow them to really whip the clubhead through the ball when they swing.

Define a strong grip. The easiest way to explain that is for you to get into your normal address position and then look down at your hands. How many of the knuckles on your left hand are visible to you? If you can see two or three knuckles, your grip is on the strong side. If you see less than two, it's on the weak side.

I take it you advocate the strong grip because, as its name implies, it will lead to greater power? For most players that would be true. If you've been a slicer and aren't happy with the distance you are getting, then I recommend that at address you rotate your left hand in your grip until you can see the first two knuckles of that hand and at least part of the third knuckle.

The stronger grip encourages "releasing" the clubhead through the ball? It's easier for the new golfer to get the kind of action with his clubhead during impact that will generate power on the shot. A stronger grip makes it possible for the toe of the club to pass the heel of the club at impact without the golfer thinking about it. This action creates a burst of clubhead speed at the bottom and that gets the distance. With a weaker grip, the toe of the club tends to lag behind the heel during impact and that causes cutting or slicing of the ball.

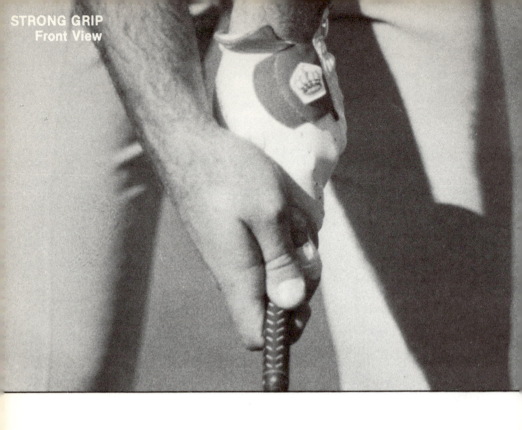

STRONG GRIP
Front View

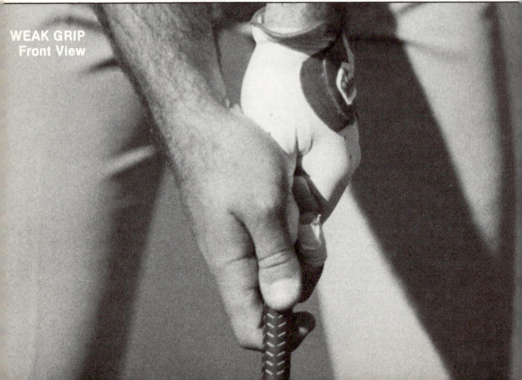

WEAK GRIP
Front View

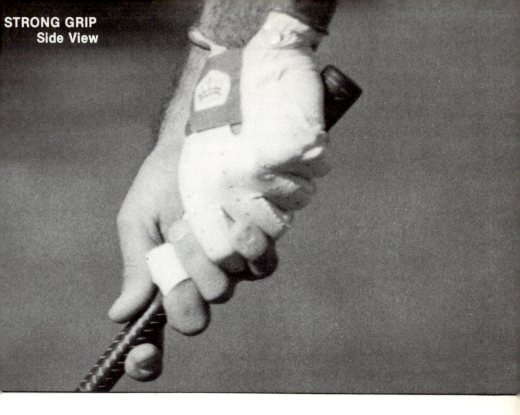

STRONG GRIP
Side View

If, in your normal address position, you see two or three knuckles on your left hand, your grip is on the strong side. If you see less than two, it's on the weak side.

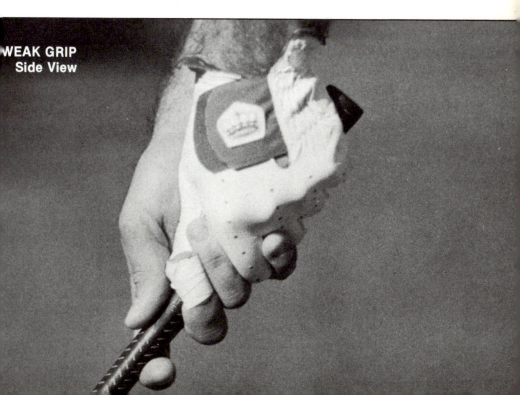

WEAK GRIP
Side View

Don't most of the touring pros have weak grips, though?

Most of the men pros do, yes. But that's because they already have great golf strength—they don't need or want to promote unfettered hand action at the bottom. But interestingly, most women pros tend to have strong grips, particularly with the left hand.

Why the difference?

Their wrists and arms are smaller and weaker than those of the men pros. They have to make an adjustment in technique to compensate for what they're lacking in physique. To get the ball out there as far as possible, they assume a stronger grip. Some of them have as many as three knuckles showing in the left hand.

The average club golfer, male or female, should copy the grips on the LPGA tour, not the men's tour, is that right?

Definitely. The person who plays golf only once or twice a week, even a robust all-American male, is unlikely to have the golf strength in his hands and arms that the male pro stars have. If he plays with a weak grip, it's going to be hard for him to draw the ball and so get the extra distance he wants. If his grip is very weak, he'll slice it all the time or even shank it. He'll be so late getting the clubface square to his target that he'll hit the ball off the hosel.

Which grip should be used, the interlock or the overlap?

Whatever you've been taught or, if you're a rank beginner, whatever feels more comfortable at the outset. I use the overlap, or Vardon, grip in which the pinkie finger of the right hand nestles in the groove between the first and second fingers of the left hand. But I don't think it's necessarily superior to the interlock, which a lot of players, Jack Nicklaus included, use. In the interlock, the first finger of the left hand is off the club handle and entwined between the fourth and fifth fingers of the right hand.

Which grip will give you more power? Neither, at least not in any significant way. I have noticed that when I am hooking the ball too much, if I change from my usual overlap to the interlock, my shots immediately straighten out. I think this happens because the interlock automatically puts my left hand in a slightly weaker position on the club handle. This suggests that the overlap may be more productive of the right-to-left pattern that allows average golfers to get more distance.

But if you're comfortable in the interlock, don't change to the overlap, and vice versa. For adding yardage, it's far more important that whatever grip you use be "dialed" to that point on the strong-to-weak compass that is right for you.

Should that dial ever be changed? It depends on how much you play. Initially, a stronger grip will help you release the club through the ball. As your hands get stronger for golf—and if you play and practice a lot, they will—you'll see you are hooking the ball too much, so you should gradually weaken your grip. Rotate the left hand back into a slightly weaker position. If you've been seeing three knuckles, cut it back to two and one half knuckles. If you've been seeing two and one half, cut it back to two.

How firmly should you hold the club in your hands? If you hold on too hard, you'll create tension in your hands and arms, which is an obvious violation of Cardinal Rule 1: Relax. But you can't hold the club as though it were a dead fish, either.

In the left hand, put on the pressure only with the last three fingers.

In the right hand, try to feel most of the pressure on the third or ring finger. The index finger and thumb of the right hand ought to be close together, pinching the club. If there's a gap between those two, your entire grip will have a tendency to slip when you take the club back.

How about going through your setting-up procedure now? First, I set the club down behind the ball, just to make sure I'm within striking range of it. You don't want to be too close to the ball or you'll shorten your swing arc and reduce your distance potential. You don't want to be too far away or you won't be able to swing in balance.

Then I set my feet so that my lower body is slightly open to the target.

What does "slightly open" mean? If my lower body were *square* to the target, an imaginary line drawn through my toes or heels would extend out to the target and remain parallel to the ball-to-target line. To make my lower body slightly *open*, that imaginary line must veer slightly to the *left* of the target line.

Are your feet perpendicular to the target line? My back foot is. My front foot is turned out slightly, toward the target, which makes it easier for me to move the clubhead through the ball on the downswing.

Back foot perpendicular to the target line, front foot turned out. What if you reversed those positions? If the back foot were turned out—toes pointing away from the target—it might be easier to take a full backswing, but I think the majority of golfers are better off starting with the front foot turned out. The challenge in golf is swinging through the ball freely, not taking the club back. If you keep that front foot angled slightly toward your target, you'll find it easier to transfer your weight to the left side, clear the hip and finish high.

How far apart should the feet be? For most people, about as far apart as the shoulders are. That will give you a solid base to turn upon. If your stance is too narrow, you can turn freely during the swing, but you'll have a tendency to sway. If you're extra wide, you can't pivot or transfer your weight.

A lot of golfers stand extra wide because it gives them the feeling they are going to hit the ball extra hard, but it actually robs you of power by fostering overhitting with the upper body instead of making a full-body swing.

Where is the ball in your stance? The ball is positioned just opposite my left heel. If you make the kind of strong drive toward the target that I recommend, that's where the ball belongs because that's where your swing will bottom out.

What if you played it back more? Then I'd have a tendency to keep my weight on the right side instead of delivering it smoothly into the shot. Many high-handicap golfers play the ball back in their stance because they fail to transfer their weight.

Okay, ball off left heel. What then?

Now I check my upper-body alignment. I want my shoulders on a line parallel to the target line. If I held a club across my chest, it would point straight out toward my goal.

Your feet are slightly open, but your shoulders are square. Why the difference?

To promote a more athletic swing. When I take the club back from this starting position, I have the feeling my upper body is working against my lower body slightly. If my stance were square, I wouldn't be able to achieve as much of a coiling effect on the backswing. With the open stance, my legs aren't turned quite as much as my shoulders are, so there's a spring-like feeling in my back muscles when the club is drawn back to the top. When I start the downswing, that gets released in a kind of springing action toward the ball. You can generate a lot more clubhead speed this way.

Is it easier or harder to make a good shoulder turn from this starting position?

It's not necessarily easier, but the shoulder turn you do make is stronger.

Are you bending from the waist in your address position?

There has to be some bend but don't hunch over or you'll limit your swing arc unnecessarily. Stand as tall as you comfortably can to take advantage of your full height.

How is the club lined up?

After I've assumed my stance, I check to make sure my left arm is an extension of the shaft of the club—that the two elements form one straight line from my shoulder all the way down to the clubhead. For this to happen and to foster a smooth, one-piece takeaway, my hands will be slightly in front of the ball. If my hands were even with the ball, my wrists would have to be bent, so you would see an angle. The trouble with the hands being even with or behind the ball is that the clubhead will lag behind when you take the club back. Then you'd have to loop the club or make some other correction to get it into a good position at the top.

Is the clubface looking directly at your target?	No, it's slightly open, meaning it is looking a bit to the right of my target. It's a visual aid for the correct takeaway. It helps me bring the club inside the line on the takeaway.
Inside the line?	My target line is the imaginary straight line going from my ball to my target. In order for me to draw the ball, I've got to swing the club back to it from inside that line on my downswing, from my side of the target line. If I start it back inside, I'll be more likely to accomplish that. If I start it back outside, I would be much more likely to slice.
How high off the ground are the hands?	The exact distance would vary with individual differences in physique. Generally, the hands should be kept on the low side because this will promote an easier, more relaxed feeling as you prepare to swing. Put the hands high and you'll feel more tension. In the lower position, the wrist joint is freer. It will help you generate better clubhead speed. In a high hand position the wrist tends to lock. You're more likely to bring the club back outside the line.

Checklist

Okay, here's what I have to do in my own setting-up procedure to develop the distance-producing draw swing:

I'm going to copy the lady pros and adopt a relatively strong grip. If I look down at the left hand in my address position, I should see at least two and maybe three knuckles. I understand that in time I may want to weaken this grip to avoid hooking the ball, but if I'm starting out as a slicer, the stronger grip will make it easier for me to bring the clubhead through on a draw-producing path.

I'm going to stand with my feet slightly open but with my shoulders square, to maximize my coiling action on the backswing.

I'm playing the ball off my left heel, hands low and slightly ahead of the ball, face of the club looking slightly to the right of target.

4 set the "explosive" on the backswing

Describe the role of the backswing. The backswing puts the club in an effective hitting position at the top. If you don't do that you're not going to hit the ball far no matter what you do on the downswing.

What are the key distance factors? The length of your swing arc, the degree of your shoulder turn and the quality of your wrist cock. These things work in combination to store up the power.

Assuming you've set up to the ball correctly, what can go wrong? Everything. You can spoil the backswing immediately by taking the club back too fast. People get quick either out of nervousness or out of the desire to hit the ball a long way. Also, you can take the club back on the wrong path.

If you want to hit the ball far, you're more prone to jump the gun at the start of the swing?

Yes, so the problem shows up most often when you're using the driver, or whenever you're trying to get all that you possibly can out of any other club.

What about nerves?

Just make sure you're not tight when you step up to hit the ball. If you feel tension in your hands or forearms, step back and take a breath. A slight forward press also will help you start the swing well.

What is a forward press, exactly?

It's a small, habitual move made just prior to taking the club back, just so you're not starting from a static address position. It could be made with practically any part of the body—Jack Nicklaus turns his head and Gary Player flexes his right knee slightly—though most commonly it's made with the hands. A slight, relaxed move of the hands toward the target serves as my forward press. It allows me to start back without tension.

What's so bad about a speedy takeaway?

The hands start back before the rest. Then it's hard for the club to catch up with the hands. For the hands and the club to be in sync on the downswing, if the club's been snatched back, some kind of extra motion or looping action has to occur at the top. This doesn't add anything in the way of power to your swing, and it makes the swing much more complicated. Usually, it's the right hand that does the snatching.

How can a golfer prevent being too quick?

Concentrate on moving the club back slowly for the first eight inches. I find that if I can get started back on the right track and in the right tempo for that short distance, my hands won't get overactive. I find that the rest of the backswing takes care of itself. The golfer is in motion at this point, so a whole lot of conscious thought is more likely to hurt than help.

Is this what is called the "one-piece takeaway"?

Yes. If your hands are set up slightly in front of the ball to begin with, then everything from shoulder joint to elbow joint to hands to shaft to clubhead goes back as one unit. I feel like I'm pushing the clubhead back along that eight-inch track with my left hand, rather than snatching it back with my right hand.

How can you prevent taking the club back on the wrong path?

The common mistake is to bring it back outside the line. Setting the club slightly open at address is a visual cue for drawing the club back slightly inside. Another way you can train yourself is to tee up a second ball about six inches behind the ball you're going to hit. You'll have to take the club back inside to avoid knocking the second ball off the tee.

What does the good hitting position at the top feel like?

I feel explosive. My shoulders have turned so fully that my back is facing the target. My left knee kicks in so that it's pointing at a spot a good 12 inches behind the ball. Not *at* the ball. Now my weight is braced on the inside of my right foot. You'll notice there's a visible quivering in my pant leg. I feel my lower body wants to move toward the target in the worst way. All I have to do is drive my legs forward to make it happen.

How far back does the club get?

I don't take it past parallel. In other words, the clubshaft is parallel to the ground when I'm at the top of my swing. The club points a little to the left of my target. If you can achieve this, or at least make that club point directly at the target, your hands will be in a more square position. If your club points to the right of target, the hands will tend to occupy a cupped position, which promotes slicing.

Why not past parallel?

I would be overtaxing my system if I did that. It puts too much strain on my hands during the downswing as I try to bring the club around in time to meet the ball squarely. Not many golfers can get away with taking the club past parallel.

Can the ordinary golfer get to this "explosive position" at the top without killing himself? Many golfers will not have the flexibility in their muscles to make a full shoulder turn or to bring the club all the way to parallel, at least not at first. If they continue to play and practice, though, they'll stretch their golfing muscles to the point where they can reach back to a power position without stress or strain.

Is the left arm straight? As straight as possible, to maximize the swing arc. But not rigid. And my left wrist is square.

What does that mean? The wrist is cocked but flat.

What's wrong with bending the wrist at the top? As the wrist goes, so goes the clubface. The square position is the one you have at address and the one you want to have at impact, when the important business gets transacted. If you let your wrist collapse into a cupped position at the top, you'll tend to hit over the top and slice the ball. If you allow it to get into a bowed position—which is a much less commonly seen fault—you'll tend to push or hook the shot.

Should the golfer be thinking about getting to that square position? Only until it comes naturally. Once it becomes an ingrained habit, you shouldn't have to think about it at all. It becomes one element among many that exists in your backswing, just one of the bricks in a well-made wall.

I'm confused about these various wrist positions. How does "cupped" and "bowed" differ from "cocked"? You can be cupped or bowed and still be cocked. The idea is to be square and cocked. Square means you can lay a ruler flat along the back of your left forearm and wrist to your knuckles. But you can be square but not cocked. If you're in the correct cocked wrist position at the top, you can see wrinkles at the base of your thumb.

Do those wrinkles disappear on the downswing? Yes, as soon as the wrist uncocks. If you imagine that you are leading the downswing with the heel of that left hand, you'll get a good picture of how that initial uncocking action should occur.

To ensure taking the club back inside the line, tee up a second ball about six inches behind your ball, as shown. To avoid hitting the second ball, you'll have to swing inside, not outside as shown at left.

You don't see those wrinkles at address?

Right. The wrist is square at address, but it's not cocked. It cocks naturally during the takeaway. My wrists are fully cocked by the time I've swung the hands back to hip height. It happens gradually as I push the club back with the left hand from my normal setup position.

Is the early wrist cock desirable for every golfer?

I think it can add to the distance you're getting. When the wrist cock is set early on the backswing, the release of the hands tends to occur later on the downswing. That delay conserves clubhead speed which is one of our power keys. But it has to happen as a by-product of the smooth, slow takeaway. If your main thought on the backswing is to cock the wrists early, your hands will get too active.

There seem to be as many technical details associated with the position at the top as there are for the setup.

The trouble with dwelling on any of them during the swing is that you may go dead in your lower body and lose your sense of rhythm. If you're overly conscious of hands and arms, especially, you'll tend to swing with little or no weight shift, or even with a reverse pivot.

What's a reverse pivot?

The golfer leans toward the target as he takes the club back. Then on the downswing, his weight falls back to the right side. He's got everything backward. Usually he'll produce a low slice with this problem.

Is it possible in the course of working on developing a better weight transfer to get too much motion?

You can lose your balance in any direction. You could sway off the ball on your backswing, fall backward on your downswing or fall forward on your follow-through. If you depart substantially from your initial address position in any of these ways, you have to work on your balance.

How?

A lot of teachers stress steadying the head position to help pupils regain their balance, without giving up their weight transfer. Try hitting a few shots in street shoes, or hit some long irons out of sand; either drill will force you to stay centered over the ball. You're talking about excessive or uncontrolled weight transfer, however, but golfers who haven't been getting good distance usually suffer from insufficient weight transfer.

Raising the left heel on the backswing helps keep your leg action supple and increases your shoulder turn.

What prevents swaying off the ball on the backswing? Shift your weight back with the idea of bracing it on the inside of the back foot. You'll be able to push off from the inside of that foot at the start of the downswing.

What's a good way to get a proper weight shift going? As knee and hips turn to the right , let the heel of your front foot lift off the ground. If you stand with that foot rooted to the ground, you're losing power unnecessarily. Lifting the heel off the ground keeps you more relaxed in your leg action, facilitates a bigger shoulder turn and allows you to get to a poised power position at the top. But remember, as the heel is lifted, the left knee must kick back, not out straight toward the ball.

Checklist

As far as the backswing goes, the three things that are going to keep me from achieving my objective of maximum length are 1) hurrying to the top, 2) limiting my shoulder turn unnecessarily and 3) forgetting to use my lower body.

I'll be more likely to take the club back with the right tempo if I remind myself that I don't need clubhead speed on the backswing, for I am not trying to hit the ball during this phase of the swing. All I'm trying to do is get the club up to a nice hitting position at the top. If I take the club away from the ball too fast, with overactive hands, I'm not going to attain that position with any consistency. If I've set up to the ball correctly, I've got a lot of things going for me already, so why ruin it with jerky tempo. All I really have to do is concentrate on taking the club back "in one piece" and slightly inside the line for the first eight inches. After that I can't do any useful thinking. I should just let the pieces fall magically in place.

I'll increase my shoulder turn by letting the left heel lift off the ground as my left knee and hips turn. The bigger the turn, the longer the swing arc. I understand that while I may not be able to take the club back to parallel in my early efforts, this will be a goal worth striving to meet because it will help me get more yardage in the long run.

I'll transfer my weight onto the inside of the back foot if I avoid becoming preoccupied with arms and hands. This isn't going to be easy because I've got a lot of interesting details to think about. So when I find myself getting overly mechanical, I should focus on lower-body action.

5 detonate downswing with lower body

What are you trying to accomplish on the downswing?
To get the greatest possible distance, two things have to happen on the downswing: good lower-body action and a delayed release of the hands. The better the leg move, the longer you can delay your hand action at the bottom, and the more clubhead speed you can save for the moment of impact when it will do the most good.

What starts the downswing?
The first move is the lower body shifting back toward the target.

The hips or the knees?
Both. You can't move one without the other. Think of it as a strong drive with your lower body toward the target.

What's wrong with starting down with the hands and arms?

If you start the downswing from topside, your arms and shoulders will spin around and the hands will follow the path of least resistance and go outside the line. You'll end up with a slice or a pull. Furthermore, you won't get your weight to the left side in time to do any good. A strong hitter would lose 25-50 yards that way.

So you're not only losing the benefit of a good weight transfer. You're also putting the club on the wrong track?

That's right. But when you work your knees toward the target properly, your hands drop farther inside the line automatically and you can bring the club down on an inside-out plane which will help you draw the ball.

But doesn't there have to be a free swinging of the club with the arms and hands?

Yes, but I want that to happen after leading with the lower body. A great baseball pitcher like Tom Seaver or Ron Guidry doesn't try to throw fast balls just with his arms. He really uses his legs to push off the mound, then lets his arm whip the ball toward the plate. In golf, the lower-body action not only gets you started down inside the line, but actually increases your potential for increasing your arm-and-hand swing speed. I really believe it's the most important key to my own swing and the biggest reason I get so much distance.

Why are so many golfers inclined to hit from the top?

Because they think that's the way they're going to get maximum distance. They try to create things to happen instead of relaxing and waiting for things to happen. This is the interval when you really have to trust the swing, otherwise you'll push the panic button. You can lack confidence in your swing and still set up to the ball and even take the club away from the ball correctly. But you can't get through the rest without trust.

How can I trust a swing that produces ground balls?

You can't pay attention to poor results if you're in the midst of building or rebuilding a swing. What does it matter if you top 10 or 20 balls in a row out on the practice range, if you're starting down correctly? Eventually you'll hit one right, and it will feel totally different from the sensations you have associated with a good swing in the past.

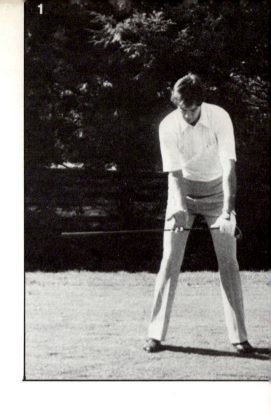

Big Cat recommends "Bill's Drill," continued on the following pages, for developing a feeling for proper hand action on the downswing. The idea is to swing the handle of the club through the impact area so it makes a whooshing sound.

Bill's Drill not only conditions the left hand to turn over properly while maintaining control of the swing, but helps develop a smooth swing tempo.

Is there any way to make that lower-body move the first thing I want to do?

It's the first thing I want to do because it relieves the strain I feel as a result of winding up my body on the backswing. If you set up to the ball as I've described and take the club back correctly, you'll feel that, too, and this should make it seem both natural and welcome for you to initiate the downswing with the lower body.

Can you consciously delay your hand action?

The more forcefully your lower body moves toward the target, the later your hands will release. If you cocked them fully by hip height on the backswing, you ought to be able to uncock them beginning no sooner than hip height on the downswing. That's a late release. But you can't consciously manipulate the hands then because there isn't enough time.

I'm confused about terminology again. What's the difference between "uncocking the wrists" and "releasing the hands"?

No difference. Both phrases are attempts to describe the desired hand action on the downswing. The wrinkles disappear at the base of your thumb as you bring the club down with the back of your hand leading. Then the left hand returns at impact to the square position it occupied at address. That gets the clubhead moving from an open position to a square one and through the ball.

The correct hand action sounds like a complicated sensation to get.

A fine teaching pro by the name of Bill Strausbaugh showed me a drill once that I think conveys exactly what the proper hand action on the downswing is. In this drill, basically, you grip the club at the clubhead end and swing the *handle* through the hitting area *(see pages 78-81).* If you do it a few times , you'll not only get a feeling for the manner in which the hands deliver the clubhead into the back of the ball at impact, but you'll establish a nice swinging tempo for yourself as well. I do the drill during a round just to stay easy and relaxed about things. The drill conditions the left hand to turn over properly and still maintain control of your swing. If you don't hear a whooshing sound at the bottom, it means the left hand hasn't released properly.

Describe a good finish position.	My weight is entirely on the left side. My belt buckle is facing the target. My hands are as high as my head and my club is pointing directly behind me.
If I finish that way, can I be sure I've made a good swing?	No, because you might be a picture poser. That's a golfer who anticipates hitting the ball, slows down the swing halfway through, then puts the club up where it belongs after the ball is long gone. The higher you can finish with your hands, the better. But you've got to let the swing put them there.
What's wrong with a short finish?	It's the trademark of ball consciousness. The worst is where your club is just pointing at the target, as though you had made a punch shot.
But isn't that the way Arnie finishes?	Arnold Palmer is so strong that he has to block his swinging motion to prevent hooking the ball. But Arnold is already out there 260-275 yards, so he doesn't need to cultivate the full finish. Club golfers interested in distance are better off copying the women pros. These players can't afford to block out their swings and cut the ball, either. So their follow-throughs are incredibly big.

Checklist

Above all, I must trust my swing to do its thing. Once I've reached my best power position at the top, I can't constructively think about mechanics, but there are a couple of things I should work on during practice to make them feel normal and comfortable to me.

I've got to start my downswing with my lower body, and not let my shoulders kill both distance and direction. My first move should be back toward the target with a smooth drive of the hips and knees. If I've wound up correctly, this first move will almost feel good because it will unspring the tension I've developed in my coil.

I've got to swing through the ball with an enthusiastic hand release. Between practice shots, I should execute Bill's Drill to remind me of the precise hand release that will square up the clubface at impact.

I've got to strive for a full LPGA Tour finish, instead of a blocking-type post-impact action, with hands up by my head and club pointing behind me. If I picture this desirable follow-through in advance of making a pass at the ball, I'll be more likely to foster a distance-producing swing-through motion and not the hit-at spasm of the bunter.

6 getting the most out of your practice

If I know I need more distance and am willing to put in the time and effort to achieve it, along the lines you've suggested, what's the first thing I should do?

Find out precisely what distance you're getting now. Go out to a golf course some evening when there's no one around and hit 20 balls. Discard the grass-cutters and infield flies and pace off the rest. Measure your stride, then count your strides. Compute the average length. Now you know where you're starting from. As I said before, most golfers don't have the foggiest idea how long they hit.

Then what? Am I supposed to incorporate into my swing all those things we've been discussing?

Well, you've got to know how to add before you can multiply. If you're a 100-shooter with a bad slice, it's not going to do you much good to be thinking about working your upper body against your lower body, say, or driving your knees toward the target. You've got to establish a base for your swing before you turn pro.

What are the priorities? Concentrate on the dynamic aspects of the swing, not the static ones. Those are the things that build up clubhead speed.

What are the dynamic aspects exactly? Get the good swinging motion, because without that you're automatically short. Then try to develop the proper draw-producing hand action. Use Bill's Drill between shots to remind yourself of the kind of releasing action you're after. Form a mental picture of the high finish position for the hands. And don't worry about where the ball goes until the motion and the hand action begin to feel natural.

After those two distance keys are established, you can pay attention to details in your setup, backswing and downswing. But take those details one at a time, or you'll get increasingly mechanical and that's going to cost you distance instead of gain it for you.

What about the grip? Assume the stronger grip right from the start, to facilitate the hand release.

Can I manage the changes all on my own? It would help to use a knowledgeable fellow golfer to check some things. It's very hard to accurately gauge your own shoulder alignment at address, for example. But it's easy for another golfer to stand behind you and say which way your shoulders are pointing. He can also tell at a glance such things as whether you're taking the club back inside the line or not, and whether you're keeping that left wrist reasonably firm and square at the top.

Where should this practice take place? A driving range.

Why is that better than on a golf course? On the course you have a tendency to steer the ball. If you're human you'll want to keep your shots in the fairway. You'll become ball conscious instead of swing conscious as a result.

On the range, there's plenty of open space and no penalties for hitting sideways, so you can concentrate on developing your basics. No one is pushing you from behind, either, so you can work on your game at a slow and steady pace.

Slow play is bad, but slow practice is good? If you machine-gun those practice balls, you won't learn anything. Make yourself think and act slowly, as though your IQ leaves something to be desired. It will help you establish better timing on the swing itself. But when you do swing, go after that ball. Let your animalistic feelings hang out a little bit. So you hit a few dead left. If you stay relaxed and keep putting a full swing on the ball, you'll begin to attain the distance you're capable of.

At the range, should I practice on a mat with its own built-in rubber tee, or should I hit off the grassy area? A mat is all right if you're working on the driver. In fact, it can help because it usually has strong vertical and horizontal lines designed into it and those will help you line up correctly. The danger in hitting off a mat is you'll tend to rush because it's so easy to tee up each succeeding ball.

Is it all right to practice with those range balls? Most ranges use balls built for durability rather than for feel or for distance characteristics, but the average golfer can practice with them quite effectively. Scratch players and pros don't like to hit range balls because in trying to compress the balls they start swinging harder than they should.

Should I practice with just the driver? No, start with short irons to get your rhythm and feel and confidence. If I hit 100 balls during a practice session, it breaks down to forty wedges and 9-irons, fifteen 7-irons, fifteen 5-irons, ten 2-irons, five 3-woods and fifteen drivers.

Would 100 balls be a good number for the average player to hit in one session? It might be better just to hit 50, especially at the start of the season. Otherwise you could get fouled up unnecessarily, by changing some of the good things that may exist in your swing simply because you're getting weary. Start with your wedge to get the flowing motion. Work up to the driver gradually, so that when you finally do get to it, you'll feel that you're swinging the club rather than forcing it. I hit more balls than average because I'm built like a giraffe and it just takes me longer to get the swing under control.

How much time should be allowed to hit a bucket of 50 balls? About an hour. If you try to squeeze your practice in between your haircut and your cocktail hour, the swing will suffer. Your metabolism has to be set on LOW to practice effectively.

A simple drill for increasing extension through the shot: Tee up your ball about six inches in front of your normal spot (left), then, without changing your setup, swing so that you still hit the ball (right).

What happens when I hit a bad shot in practice?

Back off, take a walk, perform Bill's Drill and stay even-tempered and philosophical.

What if I hit a series of bad shots?

Get even more philosophical. There are low and high cycles in any learning experience. Bear with the low ones and brag about the highs. It happens on the pro tour. Players will get on hot streaks during which they can do nothing wrong. It seems to require no thought or effort for them to hit the ball correctly. They may win three or four tournaments in a row playing that way. Then they'll start to lose it. One little gremlin will creep undetected into the swing and tilt life in favor of someone else for a while.

What about when I hit good shots?

Let the sensation of that particular swing sink in. Do an Instant Replay on your setup. Assume the exact same address position, then look down at your hands and see if you can pick out a reference point for use in the future. For instance, if I look down when I'm set up to hit my driver correctly, my view of my left knee is blocked by my left hand. That visual reference point won't be the same for other golfers, though. It could be that your left hand blocks your view of your left foot, not your knee.

The point is, by taking stock of your setup following an effective swing, you develop an awareness of where everything belongs when you're doing it right.

Are there any other drills you use on the practice tee?

My favorite after Bill's Drill is a drill for increasing your extension through the ball. It involves teeing up your ball 4 to 6 inches in front of the normal spot, then, without changing your setup, swinging so that you still hit the ball. You'll find you can improve your ability to stay down on the shot with this drill and to keep the clubhead on line through the hitting area longer.

What if I don't have time to practice a lot? The best exercise for golf is hitting golf balls. If you don't have time to do that every day, or every other day, try isometric exercises. They build the kind of wiry strength that is useful in golf, not the bulky strength that weightlifting creates and that actually hampers the swing as well as making it hard to find shirts that fit.

I did isometrics for a year back when I was in college and lengthened my tee shots 10 to 15 yards in the process. Actually, I started the exercises to help me in basketball, and they did. I improved my jumping ability by 12-15 inches—I went from just being able to reach the rim with my hand to reaching the rim with my elbow. But the real payoff came on the golf course.

Checklist

All right, you've given me some pointers for practice—and practice I must if I really do want to become the longest off the tee among my golfing friends.

The main things to remember are:

Do my duty at a driving range, not during a round. It will be easier for me to concentrate on building a dynamic, athletic swinging motion on the range because I won't be trapped into preoccupation with accuracy.

But I've got to practice at a nice peaceful rate on the range, and not dispense my bucket of balls in much less than an hour.

Whenever I hit a bad shot, I should pretend my neighbor did it, and not get rattled. If I connect on an extra-long shot, which, after all, is what I'm seeking on a regular basis, I should try to memorize the thoughts and feelings associated with it. Check out the setup from which I made that good swing, too, to find some visual reference point that I can use in assuming exactly the same stance again.

Dreary as it may sound, I must practice on a regular basis in order to stay in touch with my game and assure steady progress toward my goal. But skip the whole thing on days I have a busy schedule or if I'm in an emotional or mental traffic jam at the time. I should consider doing isometric exercises to build up my golfing muscles if I'm not able to hit balls at least twice a week.

7 the equipment edge

Can the proper equipment really help golfers get more distance?

Definitely. For example, if I have the wrong kind of shaft on my driver, I'll lose 15 yards. If I'm hitting the wrong ball, I may lose another 10 yards. Even a little thing like setting the ball on the tee the wrong way can cost me a couple of yards. So there's a total of 27 yards I'd be giving away if I didn't acknowledge the importance of equipment.

What's the right way to put the ball on the tee?

Set the ball with the brand name on top, so that its equator is running parallel to the ground. That way you'll hit on the seam where the compression, I believe, is slightly higher.

What does compression mean?

That refers to the hardness of the ball and indirectly to the amount of energy that is stored up inside. It is uniform throughout the ball, but I've discovered that I get a higher compression reading on the seam where the two halves of the ball were joined in manufacture, and the ball goes farther when I hit it there.

Assuming the golfer hits it properly? Yes. There's no sense in getting involved in minute concerns about your equipment unless you already have a solid swing to work with. Don't buy a Maserati until you pass the test for your driver's license.

After that, it's all right to get fanatical? Especially about your money clubs—the driver, putter and wedge. I'm like that with my L.D. driver.

Do you have it insured? No, Lloyd's of London quoted too high a premium. So I have to watch it like a hawk.

If you lost it, you'd be upset? Oh, yes. Most of the untold tragedies in golf have had to do with the loss of favorite clubs. I once caddied regularly for a fellow who had 47 putters in the trunk of his car with names for every one of them, names like Queenie, Silver Scot, Nicky Junior. He'd discuss the clubs the way a visitor might talk about beloved baseball players on a walk through the Hall of Fame. Whenever I carried his bag out to the car for him after a round, he'd pick up one of the putters and reminisce. "Evvie, remember Nicky Junior?" he'd say. "Remember the day we played Duke Burati and had 17 one-putt greens with Nicky Junior? And look, Evvie, the Silver Scot! Do you remember the day I used the Silver Scot to make that 12-footer on the last hole with the presses riding?"

Anyway, one day his car was stolen and he went straight into shock. It was as though his family had been wiped out in a catastrophe. He couldn't play golf again for months.

It seems that you get so you trust your favorite clubs the way you say you must trust your swing? Or maybe don't trust them. I have another friend whom I swear goes through at least 50 sets of new clubs a year. Once he teed it up in a local tournament, the Bergen (N.J.) Open. He didn't like the way he was playing after nine holes so he went into the pro shop and traded in his existing clubs for a brand new set. He didn't do much better with the new set so when he got close to the pro shop again, on the 14th hole, he went in and bought a third set. Next day in the second and final round, he went through two more sets, so he played with five different sets in 36 hours.

Isn't that against the rules? You're allowed up to 14 clubs to play a round but they're supposed to be the same ones. The point is, my friend has taken much too seriously the role equipment plays in his game.

What's the most important part of the club as far as distance goes? The shaft, because how it performs during your swing dictates the amount of clubhead speed you get. If it's too stiff it will feel like you're swinging a garden rake. The clubhead won't catch up with the hands and you'll tend to hit your shots right. If it's too flexible, it will feel more like a garden hose as you swing. The clubhead will shoot way ahead of the hands or lag way behind and you'll hit shots left and right.

How does a golfer know what flex to use? There's a choice of Ladies, Action, Regular, Stiff and Extra Stiff. The more forcefully you swing, the stiffer the shaft should be.

What do you use? I have an extra stiff shaft, the equivalent of a Double X.

How do graphite and steel compare as shaft materials? I like to use graphite because I feel as though I don't have to swing as hard, but it does take getting used to and it wouldn't be right for everyone. If you have a smooth, flowing swing, like a Gene Littler or Tommy Aaron, you'll be more likely to be able to control the graphite. If your overall motion is quicker and more forceful, in the style of an attacker like a Palmer or Trevino, then you are probably better off with steel.

Is it all right to buy the driver separately from the rest of the set? You can approach the selection of a driver the way you would pick out a utility club like the putter or wedge. The driver swing is different enough that the club you use to make it with can be judged on its own merits. It doesn't have to "match" your other clubs in feel to the nth degree.

How big is your L.D. driver? It's 44 inches long, which is one inch longer than normal, and weighs 14½ ounces, which is about 1½ ounces heavier than normal.

What's the proper overall driver weight for the club golfer?

I use a heavier club because it keeps my tempo slow. Most golfers should try for a relatively light club—in the 12-13 ounce range—because it will help them swing the club faster. That's the principle behind graphite and the new lightweight steel shafts. But they should try for a relatively heavy swingweight.

What is swingweight?

Swingweight is an expression of the distribution of the weight throughout the club. A relatively heavy swingweight indicates that the weight of the club is felt more toward the clubhead during the swing. A relatively light reading means more weight is felt at the handle end. It's an arbitrary number system related to how the club feels to the golfer.

How does the individual golfer find his or her best swingweight?

The system numbers clubs from C-1, which is very light in feel, to D-10, which is very heavy. The idea is to swing a club with as heavy a swingweight as you can, without reducing your clubhead speed. That way you have more mass behind the ball and the shot will go farther.

Remember, though, you must be able to handle the heavier swingweight up through the 18th hole of a round. A lot of people fool themselves into thinking they can handle a certain swingweight on the basis of a few swings. You've got to be as comfortable swinging the club at the end of a round as you are at the beginning.

How can I determine the swingweight on my present driver?

Any golf pro will be happy to weigh the club for you on a swingweight scale.

How can I alter the swingweight?

If you feel your present swingweight may be too light, you can put lead tape, available in any hardware store or pro shop, on the back of the clubhead. Stick a two-inch-long strip on the back side of the club, above the sole plate, and centered behind the hitting area—not too high. Then hit some balls to determine what the change feels like. Keep adding strips until you begin to consistently hit balls to the right. That means you've reached the point where the swingweight is too heavy for you to get the club through. Take the strips of tape off one at a time until you get to drawing the ball consistently.

Should the driver shaft be as long as possible?

If you can handle a driver longer than 43 inches, which is standard length, it will automatically increase your swing arc and so you should get more distance. The critical question is control—there's no sense in going to an extra-long driver if it results in the shaft swinging you. There are basic physical traits—mainly your height and the length of your arms—that must be considered in determining the best club length for you. A good PGA pro is the best person to make sure you don't ignore these.

Are there things about the clubhead itself that can affect distance?

Well, the hardness of the material used in the clubhead will influence distance to a certain extent. The best clubheads traditionally have been made out of persimmon, which is wood from an increasingly rare type of tree, or a combination of hardwoods that have been laminated together.

How can you tell you're picking out a club with a good head?

In the best persimmon clubheads, the grain runs straight or on a diagonal toward the inset, rather than in a circular pattern. If you're hitting with the grain, the ball goes farther. The best laminated clubhead types are usually found in the top line clubs—in other words, you're going to get what you pay for.

What should the loft of the driver be?

No more than 10-11 degrees. My contest driver has a 9-9½ degree loft. My playing driver has a 14-degree loft, equal to a 2-wood, but that's because I don't need all the distance I can possibly get on my tee shots in a round. But the typical golfer would sacrifice 10-30 yards by adding loft unnecessarily to his driver.

What about the grip of the club?

It's not a distance factor. Obviously, it shouldn't be too thick or too thin for your hand size. Whether you use leather or composition grips is a matter of personal preference.

Are golf shoes a distance factor?

The distance-producing swing we've been talking about puts a lot of emphasis on lower-body action and footwork. So I would say it is essential to have quality, well-fitting shoes with spikes that are sharp. If you have worn-out spikes on your shoes you won't have as good a hold on the planet during the swing.

What golf ball can I get the most yardage with? Any ball that meets USGA specifications has certain velocity limits designed into it, so you can't really buy distance over the counter. But there are variations in the construction and compression of balls that permit a smart golfer to pick up yardage by using the right ball for his swing and for the playing conditions at the time.

What's the difference between solid balls and wound balls? Solid balls are made of a durable synthetic plastic material called Surlyn. They'll last longer than wound balls because they won't nick or cut. But they come off the clubface faster so you can't put as much spin on them. This means they won't check up as much on the turf when they land. You could get more roll out of them on hard fairways, but you'd have a harder time making your approach shots stop on small greens.

The wound ball has a thin balata cover and a mile or so of thin rubber band wound around a liquid center. Balata is a softer material than Surlyn, so it cuts more easily, but that is also why it stays on the clubface longer, giving you greater spin and control, especially with irons.

A third type of ball increasingly popular today combines the best characteristics of both these balls. It comes with a Surlyn cover, which makes it more durable for the average player, and a wound liquid center, which gives it more of the playability of a balata-wound ball.

Which type goes farther in the wind? With the driver, the balata-covered wound ball goes farther, against the wind or with the wind. A good solid ball may go almost as far into the wind, but it won't fly as far downwind. With long irons into the wind, a good solid ball with small dimples will go farther than a wound ball. It'll bore into the wind. There'll be less spin on the ball, and therefore a little less control, but great precision isn't usually the main job of long irons.

So the dimple pattern on a ball affects distance? Balls with small dimples generally carry 10 percent farther into the wind. Balls with large dimples do 10 percent better with the wind, because they'll fly on a higher trajectory. Conceivably, you could carry both types of balls around on a blowy day and on each hole tee off with the type that will fly better in the conditions present.

How does ball compression affect distance? Balls are manufactured with compressions ranging from 50 to 100. Driving ranges use 50-compression balls because they last longer. Pro shops basically offer you a choice among 80, 90 and 100 compression balls. The higher the compression, the firmer your swing action has to be. If you can't fully compress the ball, you're not releasing all its stored-up energy. The average golfer will get more distance by fully compressing an 80 or 90 compression ball than by trying to hit a 100 compression ball and only partially compressing it.

Is it true that balls just don't travel as far in cold weather? Definitely, but you can cut your losses by changing to lower compression balls when the weather turns. If it gets below 50 degrees Fahrenheit, drop to the next lower range of compression—if you've been hitting 90's, switch to 80's. You'll still lose some yardage, compared to your hot-weather performance, but not as much.

At what point would you feel golfers might be getting too esoteric about their equipment concerns? You can go overboard, sure. If you spend most of your round on a windy day thinking about ball compression and dimple size and such, you probably won't play very well or with as much enjoyment, which is even more important. On the other hand, after you reach a certain level of proficiency, there are equipment decisions you can and should make because they'll add yards to your drives.

Playing with the club or ball that you know permits you to produce your longest shots also has a psychological value. For that matter, you should not ignore your intuitive or esthetic or even downright superstitious tendencies. For example, I feel more confident hitting No. 4 balls in long driving contests because that was the number on the ball I hit to win my first contest. I realize that a No. 4 ball will not travel any farther than a No. 3 ball of the same type from the same manufacturer and hit with the same golf swing. But if playing the No. 4 ball makes me feel happier, more relaxed and more sure of myself, why should I deny myself those advantages?

Checklist

Summing up, the most important equipment consideration as far as getting distance off the tee is my choice of driver. The main things to bear in mind:

1. Try for the lightest possible overall club weight right for me, in order to facilitate swinging with good speed.

2. Try for the heaviest possible swingweight right for me, so I have maximum mass behind the ball at the bottom of my swing.

3. Find the degree of flexibility in my shaft that is suitable to the amount of force I am able to generate when I swing.

As far as golf balls go, the main distance factors are:

1. Construction—balata-covered wound balls generally go farther than solid balls.

2. Compression—I should play the ball—80, 90, or 100 degree compression—that I can fully compress with my normal swing. If 90 is right for me, I'll lose potential yardage if I over-compress an 80, or under-compress a 100.

3. Dimple pattern—balls made with larger-than-normal dimples generally fly better with the wind, but could lose yards for me into the wind.

I have to build a good swing before changes in equipment will make any difference in the distance I am getting. However, in working on my swing, I should have a driver that fits my physique and basic swinging strength, so I ought to get this item cleared with a good pro before I proceed.

BIG CAT
AND CHIEFIE
AT OAKMONT

a long drive
drama in five
short acts

1 working out at 9-W

Time: One month prior to the annual National Long Driving Contest, put on by *Golf Digest Magazine* and the PGA and held in conjunction with the PGA Championship, in 1978 at Oakmont.

Scene 1: 9-W Golf Range, George Kopac, Prop. Location, 20 miles north of Manhattan on New York State Highway 9-W. Midday. Clear summer sky.

Evan Williams, a.k.a. Big Cat, 30 years old, 6 feet 6 inches, 205 pounds, has been on the mats for half an hour, trying to break in the new graphite shaft in his contest driver, but he is still leaving everything a little bit right, suggesting that the shaft may be too stiff for him. He pauses from time to time to wipe the sweat and consternation off his face.

He is practicing at 9-W because it is one of the few ranges in the metropolitan area spacious enough to accommodate his plus-300-yard drives. Other ranges refuse to let him hit wood shots because they say the balls don't come back.

Also, Big Cat happens to be friends with the owner of 9-W, a man who swings a mean driver himself. George Kopac is so strong that the tattoos on his forearms have muscles, and his reflexes are good enough that he can take the club 20 degrees past parallel and still get it back in time to pound the ball squarely, average length of drive, 290 yards.

Presently, George Kopac is watching, not hitting. Arms folded, he straddles Big Cat's target line and watches.

KOPAC: *(after Big Cat hits yet another shot to the right)* Tell you what, I think maybe you're taking it back outside.
BIG CAT: *(frowning)* You think so?
KOPAC: I think that's what you're doing.
BIG CAT: Could be. I tend to jerk it back outside the line when I'm trying to let it eat.
KOPAC: *(puzzled)* "Let it eat?"
BIG CAT: That's what the touring pros say when they want to hit it far. *(addressing next ball)* Tell me if I take it back inside this time.
KOPAC: *(after Big Cat hits)* That was better. *(watching ball rise)* Much better tempo. *(still watching ball)* Oh, you caught that good. *(still watching)* Hmmm. *(Ball finally enters woods on the fly.)* You definitely let that one eat.
BIG CAT: *(grins)* That could win L.D. IV!

Scene 2: 9-W Range, 15 minutes later.

Kopac has returned to duties inside his shop. Big Cat has put up his 44-inch-long driver and moved left two mats to observe the golf swing of another friend named George.

This is George Berkner, a 38-year-old professional horse trainer and harness racer who rode up from Jersey in Big Cat's Cougar this day.

Berkner took up golf two years ago. Recently, under Big Cat's guidance, he has transformed his primeval slice swing pattern into a flowing, inside-out swing that is beginning to yield long and straight tee shots. If emotions ruled his life, George Berkner would drop everything and go on the PGA tour starting tomorrow.

BERKNER: *(after producing a 230-yard drive)* Just look at that, can you believe it?
BIG CAT: You're doing it, George. You've got that swinging motion. You're finishing like a human.
BERKNER: Never in all my days have I hit a ball better, Big Cat.
BIG CAT: You've got it, George!
BERKNER: *(hits another)* That ball is actually going from right to left!
BIG CAT: You are *drawing* the ball, George, just like they do in the movies!
BERKNER: I am a happy man, Big Cat. I am a fulfilled person right now, thanks to you. *(tees up another ball and tops it)* Well, I *was* fulfilled.

Scene 3: Same place, a few minutes later.

A gleaming red and silver 750-cc Triumph Bonneville motorcycle skids into the gravel parking lot of the 9-W Range and twists to a halt in a cloud of dust. Aboard is a 30-year old male dressed in blue cord suit, striped tie and white helmet embossed with butterflies. He unstraps the helmet, places it on the bike seat and moves in the direction of George Kopac's snack bar operation, called "The Sand Wedge." But he stops in his tracks when he catches sight of Big Cat, who is listlessly puffing on a Marlboro, himself still watching George Berkner crank out his best-ever drives. He spreads his arms wide and starts toward Big Cat in a menacing stride last seen in the wrestling ring in the person of Argentina Rocca.

CHIEFIE: I don't believe my eyes, not either of them! *(As he nears Big Cat, Chiefie shifts into a tone of voice best described as sports-announcer-ese.)* IT IS EVAN "THE BIG CAT" WILLIAMS, PRIDE OF LEONIA, A LIVING LEGEND IN HIS OWN LIFETIME, A FABULOUS FOUR-LETTER PHENOM FROM LITTLE KNOWN FRANKLIN COLLEGE, THE GARDEN STATE'S VERY OWN, OUR GIFT TO GOLF, TWO-TIME LONG DRIVE CHAMPION OF THE WORLD, HIMSELF, IN PERSON. . . .anyway, how are you, Big Cat!

BIG CAT: Chiefie, where in hell did you come from? George, stop holding that finish for the Associated Press and look here. *(Big Cat also switches into sports-announcer-ese.)* LADIES AND GENTLEMEN, NOW ON THE TEE, FROM ENGLEWOOD GOLF CLUB, PLAYING TO AN INFLATED HANDICAP OF 17, DRESSED AS USUAL LIKE A DROPOUT FROM YALE, IT IS THE INCREDIBLE CHIEFIE! *(Big Cat and Chiefie shake hands and slap shoulders.)* Chiefie, it has been *years.* You live up this way now?

CHIEFIE: I still live in Jersey where I used to, you just haven't been in touch since you got world famous. Clinics, exhibitions, endorsements, write-ups in *Golf Digest, Sports Illustrated,* network TV, all the things I always predicted for you, all come true. So what are you doing now?

BIG CAT: Practicing for Oakmont.

CHIEFIE: For L.D. IV!

BIG CAT: *(to George)* He says it in Roman numerals, George, like it's the Superbowl.

CHIEFIE: It is! The Long Drive is on a level with your Masters or your Indy 500 now.

BIG CAT: I want you to meet my friend George Berkner. *(George and Chiefie shake.)* Chiefie and I were caddies together, George. He always told me I had a future.

BERKNER: Can you sue him for libel?

BIG CAT: *(laughs)* George here is knocking the ball pretty good, Chiefie.

BERKNER: I am in nirvana!

CHIEFIE: Is that down by Trenton?

BIG CAT: *(pushing Chiefie)* C'mon Chiefie, where's your mind today? Actually, George here is one hell of a jockey. Ran BG's Bunny to a new world record last year at the Meadowlands.

CHIEFIE: Aren't you kind of big for a jock?

BIG CAT: George rides *pacers,* Chiefie. HARNESS RACER AND HORSE TRAINER EXTRAORDINAIRE, MR. GEORGE BERKNER. A sulky turned over on him five years ago and snapped his collarbone in six places. That's why he's got a big loop in his backswing.

CHIEFIE: All the ponies I bet on have been going down the toilet lately, George. You wouldn't have anything good coming up?

BERKNER: I like Big Cat at Oakmont.

BIG CAT: Chiefie, forget the tips on horses, huh? Tell me what you're up to these days?

CHIEFIE: I got a job in a warehouse, Big Cat. Not far from here. I'm in charge of a shitload of small appliances.

BIG CAT: You go to work in a warehouse all dressed up?

CHIEFIE: Sure. Hey, I have my own style. Comes to dressing proper, Chiefie is there first and foremost, case closed.

BIG CAT: You come out here for lunch?

CHIEFIE: I sit here in the sun and watch the players and think about the old days, like when we played Englewood backward under cover of night, or the time you took out the picture window in the big red house on the 17th fairway, or that day you got the phone call in the caddieyard, which was Red Holzman asking you on bended knee to please try out for the Knicks, and you turn the man down!

BIG CAT: I knew I wanted to be a *golfer* by then!

CHIEFIE: Or sometimes I skip lunch and tool up to a little place north of here where I have a lady in waiting, believe it or not. That's a change from the old days, ain't it? Someone who waits for me instead of visa reversa.

BIG CAT: *(to George, who has resumed hitting balls)* Poor Chiefie here holds the high school world record for number of times stood up!

CHIEFIE: But my luck has changed, Big Cat.

BIG CAT: What's your secret with the lady up north?

CHIEFIE: Small appliances, Big Cat. I get her all she wants, marked down 100 percent, you know? But never mind my colorful love life. Let me see you hit a few live ones. NOW ON THE TEE, FROM LEONIA, NEW JERSEY. . . .

Scene 4: Half hour later.

Hudson Terrace, five miles north of 9-W Range. This is a friendly working-class bar with air conditioning, pinball machine, handwritten supper menu, family photographs on the wall, several wooden Indians and a three-star view of the Hudson River and the Tappan Zee Bridge, which spans the river gracefully, like an approach shot to an island green.

Big Cat and Chiefie have their backs to the view and beers in front of them. George, who is due to race at Monticello late that night, is working on a 7-Up. All watch "Newsbreak," which is presently reporting on an ice cream truck explosion in the busy Wall Street district earlier that day. The blow-up has injured dozens of pedestrians and caused much property damage.

WOMAN BEHIND THE BAR: Mafia are everywheres!

MAN AT BAR, WITH FACE LIKE THE BATTLEFIELDS OF VERDUN:
Mmmmmghgmmmmhn!

CHIEFIE: I agree with both of you. Why don't we see if we can find some
sports?

BIG CAT: Chiefie, you work Saturdays?

CHIEFIE: Some Saturdays. It depends.

BIG CAT: I got an exhibition to do in Philadelphia in a couple of weeks. If you
want to ride down with me, you're welcome. Assuming you can get off
from work.

CHIEFIE: *(beaming)* Can I get off from work to join the Big Cat in Phillie? Is
Paris still in France? Do birds fly? Is the Pope Catholic? Are the Mets in
last place? Count on me, Big Cat.

BIG CAT: Should I count on him, George?

BERKNER: *(finishing his 7-Up)* Count on the guy!

2 the sectionals at Philly

Time: Two weeks prior to L.D. IV.

Big Cat arrives at Hi-Point Golf Farm, an attractive public golf complex outside of Philadelphia. He is alone—Chiefie could not get off from work after all. He has a new shaft in his contest driver and it is working much better for him than the one he experimented with at 9-W.

The July sun glitters in the tassels of the shoulder-high corn in the fields surrounding the course. It is so hot the begonias and impatiens are wilting in the shade. Some of the golfers roam the course affecting the caveman look, tee shirts off.

Scene 1: The Hi-Point Snack Shoppe.

Resident pro Tom Smith buys Big Cat a cheeseburger. Smith will emcee the exhibition and the Long Drive Sectional Qualifier to follow, during which 31 golfers will compete for three spots at Oakmont. A total of 15 PGA sections are holding similar qualifiers throughout the country this day, having previously winnowed down the year's total L.D. field of more than 3,000 amateur and professional sluggers. As defending champion, Big Cat is exempt from all this, and has come down primarily as a favor to Golf Digest and to promote the Long Drive generally because it raises money for PGA junior golf programs. And also because he didn't have anything better to do.

SMITH: I appreciate your making the trip. I really believe this is the kind of event we need. Golf is standing still in this country right now. If we all get behind it, the Long Drive will get a lot more people excited about the game.

BIG CAT: It's different, isn't it?

SMITH: Making short putts is important as hell, but hitting long drives is what turns people on.

BIG CAT: Well, that's what I came for.

SMITH: How long do you think you can give us? Ten minutes?

BIG CAT: Make it at least a half an hour.

Scene 2: The 10th tee at Hi-Point is the site selected for both exhibition and Sectional Qualifier. A crew armed with two-way radios and tape measures is stationed way down on the straight par-4 fairway. Lines have been drawn football-field style at 10-yard intervals from 250 to 350 yards. A large crowd gathers as Tom Smith introduces "the longest hitting golf pro in the world."

Big Cat steps out, tells the gallery what a great job Tom Smith has been doing, and proceeds through a 30-minute routine in which he hits 45 balls, narrates seven funny stories, cracks five one-liners, and answers 20 questions about swing technique. In condensed form:

BIG CAT: (at the outset, after spending five minutes explaining the whys and wherefores of his setup) Well, I haven't missed a fairway yet!

GALLERY: Hoo! Ha! Ha!

BIG CAT: (after hitting a shot that carries 165 yards) That's my 9-iron.

GALLERY MEMBER: (sotto voce) That's Howie's drive.

HOWIE: (loudly) Shuddup.

BIG CAT: (laconically, after hitting a shot that carries 200 yards) 5-iron.

ANOTHER GALLERY MEMBER: 5-iron? I'm quitting this goddam game.

BIG CAT: (after pushing one into the spruce trees on the right) By the way, I'm working on a book. It's going to be called, "101 Ways to Chip Back into the Fairway."

GALLERY: Ha, ha! Hee! Haw haw!

BIG CAT: It's a sequel to my first one, "Power Shanking."

GALLERY: Ha! etc.

BIG CAT: (after rifling a few 300-yarders) Well, that's the 2-iron.

GALLERY MEMBER: Jeez!

ANOTHER GALLERY MEMBER: Big Cat, have you ever played anybody who's out-hit you?

BIG CAT: On one hole maybe. (pause) But never all day.

Big Cat finally works up to his contest driver, at which point the chatty and relaxed atmosphere in the crowd suddenly goes away. The people still enjoy Big Cat's easy manner, so it must be the consistently awesome drives he now produces that create a certain tension among them, and elicit groans, sighs and whimpers instead of appreciative giggles and laughs. The gallery begins to sound like a chorus in a Greek tragedy.

GALLERY: λαιδρη κορωνη, κως το χειλος

Scene 3: Same location, shortly after conclusion of Big Cat's show. Pro/emcee Smith still at the mike. Same gallery, holding refills of beer and soda.

SMITH: *(via the resonant P.A. system set up for the occasion)* On the tee, please, our first contestant, Matt Panos from Westport, Connecticut. *(for the next two hours, 29 of the 31—there are two no-shows—Sectional Qualifiers will hit balls in the general direction of the 40-yard-wide fairway—some of the more nervous types being substantially left or right of the goal. The format is: each golfer gets to hit four balls, then waits his turn to hit four more balls again. The three golfers who produce the longest drives in fair territory get to go to Oakmont in two weeks. The competition starts on a slight snag as the teeing area remains deserted in spite of Smith's introduction of the first contestant.)* Matt Panos, where are you? *(another long pause, tee still empty, spectators looking at each other)* Anyone seen Matt Panos? *(after another minute, a harried-looking young man breaks from the crowd and bounds up on the tee)* I should remind you, Matt Panos, you have a time limit. *(Panos drops his four balls on the turf)* There's no hurry, understand, but please don't tarry. *(Panos searches all his pockets for a tee, finally locates one, then hits his shots.*

PANOS: *(after hitting fourth and last ball)* #!??#$!#&#!!

SMITH: *(after listening on earphone for confirmation from the crew down the fairway for results that were fairly apparent from the tee)* All four balls by Matt Panos were out of play. Next on the tee. . . .

As the contest proceeds, Big Cat mingles with the contestants. Most of them are handsome young studs with shoulder turns so big they would be sung about if only Carly Simon or Linda Ronstadt knew anything about golf. A few ask Big Cat questions, usually about equipment.

CONTESTANT: Do you really think you get more out of the graphite, Big Cat?

BIG CAT: It gives me better timing. I have the feeling I don't have to swing as hard. But it might not produce the same results for you.

SECOND CONTESTANT: Big Cat, I cut down the loft on my driver to seven degrees, so I could get more roll.

BIG CAT: Gee, I would do just the opposite, you know? Add loft so you get more carry.

THIRD CONTESTANT: Hey, Big Cat, what would you think of my chances if I got me a 45-inch driver?

BIG CAT: You'll hit it farther but not as straight.

FOURTH CONTESTANT: I'd like to x-ray those balls you use.

BIG CAT: *(slightly peeved)* Go right ahead! *(more relaxed)* There's nothing special about them. In fact, the ones I hit today are out of the shag bag. I've been practicing with them for a month. They're practically rocks!

Toward the end of the first round appears one Steve Sweet, a 6 foot 9 inch, off-speed golfer from Big Cat's hometown, known to friends as "Jabar." After several announcements of his Christian name by Smith, Jabar stumbles up on the tee carrying his spikes and two drivers. Hastily he changes into his shoes. He is wearing checked polyester slacks cut off above the knee and a tee shirt saying BOOTH'S GIN. Like Matt Panos, the late-coming first contestant, Jabar hits his four balls O.B., all way right. Immediately he seeks solace with Big Cat.

JABAR: Cripes, how can they rush people like that!

BIG CAT: Jabar, you got to try to be on time for these things!

JABAR: I did try! I got the wrong directions. I was all the way into Philadelphia. I saw the freaking Liberty Bell!

BIG CAT: Don't worry about all that any more, Jabar. You have four more balls to hit, remember, and any one of them can put you in the running for Oakmont. Just relax and wait it out and then put your best swing on it.

But 45 minutes later, Jabar performs poorly again. Shortly after that, the Qualifier is over.

SMITH: *(still at the mike)* Today's leading qualifier is Dirk Zuhlke with a drive of 311 yards, 2 feet. *(applause)* I'd like to add that the longest drive hit in the fairway by Evan Williams during his exhibition earlier was measured at 345 yards even. *(applause, hoots, cries and whistles)* Let me say this, I've seen Long Jimmy Thompson, who was a hulk of a man, and Craig Wood, who hit some mighty drives in his time, and George Bayer, who was 300 pounds of muscle in motion, but I've never watched any golfer bang them out there quite like Big Cat. I want to thank him again·for joining us today. *(applause, as Big Cat grins and waves from among the crowd)* Obviously, you are ready for Oakmont!

3 long drive eve

Time: Tuesday of PGA Championship Week, the day before L.D. IV. The action occurs in and around Oakmont Country Club, the tournament site, located outside Pittsburgh, Pa. Particulates Count for the air in this area for the week, according to local weather reports, is 135, "Unhealthful."

Scene 1: Late afternoon. Holiday Inn, Harmarville, five miles from Oakmont.

Chiefie arrives on his Triumph Bonneville with its tear-drop shaped tank. After seven hours on the road, his blue cord suit is slightly rumpled, his loafers and white athletic socks are covered with soot, and he has bugs on his teeth. He unsuccessfully rings Big Cat's room, then goes to the front desk.

CHIEFIE: I'd like a room, thank you, two nights.
ROOM CLERK: I'm sorry, sir, we're full right up. The PGA is in town.

Scene 2: Howard Johnson's Motor Lodge, Monroeville, 15 miles from Oakmont.

CHIEFIE: I would like to check in.
ROOM CLERK: Do you have a reservation? We're awful busy right now. The
    PGA. . . .
CHIEFIE: I know, I know. Just give me a room, any room. I don't even require
    fresh stationery.

Scene 3: Room 202, Howard Johnson's Motor Lodge, Monroeville. For
10 minutes, Chiefie studies the motel's intricate instructions on how to use the
phone, then dials the Holiday Inn in Harmarville. Still no answer in Big Cat's
room. Chiefie leaves a message: "The Chief is here to lend moral support as
needed. Please get in touch when you return."
    Chiefie feeds two quarters into his vibrating mattress and lays back on the
bed, hoping the treatment will persuade some of the Pennsylvania Turnpike
to leave his spine.

Scene 4: Early evening. Room 185, Holiday Inn, Harmarville.

CHIEFIE: I hope I'm not imposing on you, Big Cat.
BIG CAT: Are you kidding? I'm glad you could get off work.
CHIEFIE: I didn't exactly get off work, I quit. I told them I had to see the big
    Cat win L.D. IV and if they wouldn't let me have a couple of days off, they
    could take their small appliances and shove them.
BIG CAT: We'll go to a movie, then have a couple of beers. I don't want to go
    to bed too early, you know? The contest doesn't start until 5 P.M.
    tomorrow. I want to have a good sleep, get up real late, so by the time it
    starts, I'll still be feeling fresh.
CHIEFIE: *(picking up Gideon Bible which lays open on a table)* How come you
    got this turned to "The Book of Job?"
BIG CAT: *(shrugs)* That's how it was when I got here, I guess.
CHIEFIE: "The Book of Job" is not your best possible good-luck sign.
BIG CAT: Why not?
CHIEFIE: Job is the guy who never makes out. He is the Charlie Brown of
    the Old Testament. *(flipping pages)* We got to find something more upbeat
    for the Big Cat. *(still flipping)* How about "Song of Solomon?" *(reading)*
    "To the steeds of Pharaoh's chariots would I liken you. . . ."

Scene 5: A shopping center cinema complex between Monroeville and
Harmarville.
    Big Cat and Chiefie arrive and buy tickets for the one of four different main
features available that happens to be scheduled to start in a few minutes.
Neither catches the coincidental logic in the title of this movie, "The Driver,"
until several minutes after the show is under way.

BIG CAT: *(in the aisle seat to better accommodate his long legs)* Hey, Chiefie, this movie is called "The Driver!" How do you like that?

CHIEFIE: *(sputtering through popcorn)* Now that's what I consider a good sign, Big Cat! THAT IS A GOOD SIGN!

THEATER PATRON: Shhhh!

"The Driver" is the story of a professional getaway-car operator. Ryan O'Neal plays the title role with the expressiveness of a smooth stone. But there are several cops-and-robbers chase scenes that Big Cat and Chiefie greatly enjoy, so the flick serves its purpose.

Scene 6: At movie's end, Big Cat and Chiefie repair to the bar at the Howard Johnson's in Monroeville and order beers. It is so dark in there people can't see their own swizzle sticks, but some of them recognize Big Cat anyway.

BARTENDER ONE: Hey, Big Cat, my buddy is the starter out there at Oakmont.

BIG CAT: Is that so?

BARTENDER ONE: Are you ready to win it again?

CHIEFIE: He's ready!

BIG CAT: I'm ready.

BARTENDER TWO: *(shaking Big Cat's hand)* We met down in Orlando.

BIG CAT: *(tentative)* Yeah?

BARTENDER TWO: At the "Why Not" Bar.

BIG CAT: That place!

BARTENDER: Right! If you can't pick up something there, leave Florida.

BIG CAT: For your information, Chiefie, the "Why Not" bar is a well-known singles bar. Even you could make out.

CHIEFIE: I doubt that. *(musing)* I suppose female companionship would not be desirable on a night like this?

BIG CAT: Well, that would depend on where the scratch marks are. But it is true you can't always take the club back as far the next day.

CHIEFIE: *(grinning)* And you're ready to take the club all the way back tomorrow, right, Big Cat?

BIG CAT: Everything's going just perfect. I thought we had a problem earlier today when I was told the long drive contestants would not be able to hit drivers off the practice tee out at the course. The practice area isn't that big at Oakmont, see, and they were saying we would be too long for it. That would be a disadvantage, you know—not being able to warm up properly before the contest. It's bad enough they won't give us lockers.

CHIEFIE: So what did you do?

BIG CAT: So I talked to a few people in the PGA and they decided they would let us hit woods off the tee after all, which is only fair.

CHIEFIE: When E. F. Cat talks, people listen.

BIG CAT: *(after a pause)* But I really want to win that thing tomorrow, Chiefie. Three in a row. . . .

CHIEFIE: Case closed, there's no one in the country who can put it past your best knock. The champagne will be on me.

BIG CAT: Do that. Bring over a bottle of champagne right away if I win, so I have it there when they make the award and the reporters start asking me what is the meaning of life. That's what Tony Lema would order after a big win.

Big Cat and Chiefie order a second round. A disco band starts up and some couples promptly move under the lights and begin to dance as if human corkscrews. Friends and golf writers come over and try to chat with Big Cat in the din, then wander off.

CHIEFIE: *(shouting in order to be heard)* You're a celebrity, you know that?
BIG CAT: *(also shouting)* No, I'm not! A celebrity is someone who is recognized outside his special field. Arnold Palmer is a celebrity. He doesn't have to be on a golf course or with golfers to be recognized. He could go live among the Sioux and everyone would still know who he was.
CHIEFIE: The who?
BIG CAT: The *Sioux.* Now the next rung down from that would be your Famous Person. The F.P. is someone who is recognized only within his special field. George Berkner—remember the guy you met out at the driving range a few weeks ago? He is an F.P. wherever harness racing takes place. But he's not a celebrity like Arnie. The Sioux wouldn't know who the hell George was.
CHIEFIE: And where does the Living Legend fit into all this?
BIG CAT: The Living Legend is a concept that exists only in the mind of a good friend. *(pause)* Do you want one more for the road, Chiefie? I'll tell you, I'm really glad you came all this way to keep me company.
CHIEFIE: Whatchasay?
BIG CAT: Forget it! Watch the dancers!

4 view from a fork-lift

Time: Wednesday of PGA Championship week, and the day of L.D. IV.

Scene 1: Chiefie, claiming he is a relative of Chris Schenkel, is permitted to hop inside a PGA Courtesy Car outside his motel. This he expects will take him promptly out to Oakmont to meet Big Cat.

The courtesy car is driven by a fiftyish woman wearing a green and white poly-cotton outfit designed to make her and all the other tournament volunteers look cute, casual and efficient. The woman is pleasant enough but, in attempting a shortcut out to the course, she gets lost, and Chiefie sees more countryside than he bargained for.

After the first hour, the courtesy car driver begins to pause regularly on her journey to ask for directions from local geographers among the road-paving crews and the people selling zucchini squash at roadside stands.

During all this, Chiefie practices a form of Transcendental Meditation by crossing his eyes and focusing on the hood ornament of the car.

Scene 2: Two and a half hours later.

DRIVER: *(gaily)* Well, we finally made it! I am truly sorry for the delay! Have a good day!
CHIEFIE: Many thanks, many thanks.

Chiefie finds Big Cat behind the clubhouse talking to several black men wearing white coveralls.

CHIEFIE: What is this, a convention of nurses' aides?
BIG CAT: These are my main men, Chiefie! The caddies! Where've you been anyway?
CHIEFIE: I'm not sure, but I think I was in the Poconos. The courtesy car got lost. I should've taken my bike.
CADDIE: *(looking Chiefie up and down)* You telling me you got a *motor*cycle?
CHIEFIE: Came all the way from New Jersey on it.
SECOND CADDIE: Whatsit, man?
CHIEFIE: 1975 Triumph, 1500 cc.
CADDIE: Pshsssssshhhh!
CHIEFIE: What's that supposed to mean?
CADDIE: That ain't no bike.
SECOND CADDIE: That's hardly a tricycle what you got!
THIRD CADDIE: I heard 1975 was a bad year for them Triumphs, anyway. They all been *re*called!
BIG CAT: *(taking Chiefie's arm)* C'mon, before you get all of us in trouble.
CHIEFIE: *(calling back over his shoulder)* Got me here!
THIRD CADDIE: *(to Big Cat)* You be large today!
BIG CAT: I will!
FOURTH CADDIE: We be waiting here after!
BIG CAT: Beers on me if I win!
SECOND CADDIE: We be waiting all right. But leave that boy in the stripey suit somewheres behind you, Big Cat. He got too much class for us.

Scene 3: Big Cat and Chiefie wander around to the crowded 18th green area which is a veritable crocus patch of colorful shirts and blazers.

BIG CAT: I'm going to get my clubs out of the car. They said we could start using the practice tee at 2:30 and it's almost that time.
DAVE MARR: *(former PGA champ and current TV commentator, approaching from practice green where he has been chatting with touring pros)* Hey, Short Knocker!
BIG CAT: How you doing, Dave! You going to be out there later?
DAVE MARR: We're all plugged in and ready to go. How you feeling?
BIG CAT: Never better. Hey, listen, I hope we give you guys a good show today.
DAVE MARR: We're looking forward to it. Got to go!
BIG CAT: Good luck behind that mike!
DAVE MARR: See you at 5, Big Cat!

CHIEFIE: Damn, you know everybody!
BIG CAT: Let's head for the practice range.

On the way, they stop at Big Cat's car. He opens the trunk and takes out his bag of clubs. He wraps a thin adhesive gauze around the third finger of his right hand, where he has a tendency to blister. He tries two brand new white, small-medium gloves, and decides the first one fits him better.

Scene 4: Oakmont practice range.
Big Cat, Cotton Dunn (last year's L.D. runner-up) and several other contestants walk out on the practice tee. Many of the touring pros who have been practicing are calling it a day right about now. Lee Trevino gives an interview on Mutual Broadcasting System. He stands there all asweat and effortlessly produces Great Radio. Elsewhere Tom Watson sits down to review the typewritten version of a short piece he has dictated on junior golf for *Golf Digest*, then plunges into a throng of four-foot-high autograph seekers.
Chiefie watches from the other side of the snow fencing that has been set up to keep the populi from interfering with the backswings of the pros. Near Big Cat and Cotton Dunn, he sees two men, one in a PGA blazer and one with a two-way radio, confer. Moments later he sees Big Cat's expression change and he knows something has gone wrong. He approaches for a closer listen.

MAN ON TWO-WAY RADIO: One of my workers down here just got hit by a
    ball. It's not safe for the long drive contestants to use woods down here.
    They can hit irons, but that's all. I'm sorry.
MAN IN BLAZER: You long drive contestants—no wood clubs, please!

Chiefie watches as Cotton Dunn borrows an iron out of Big Cat's bag to hit with; he brought nothing but his driver down to the range, under the impression he would be allowed to use it.
Chiefie watches Big Cat shank his first shot with a pitching wedge. Never in all his days, not since they were looping together at Englewood, has Chiefie seen Big Cat shank a wedge. So he knows Big Cat is upset.
A few minutes later, Big Cat throws his bag on his shoulder and leaves the tee.

BIG CAT: Let's go.
CHIEFIE: Where?
BIG CAT: Down the road. I got to hit some drivers.
CHIEFIE: Who was that idiot on the walkie-talkie?
BIG CAT: Don't call him that, Chiefie! The man's been club pro here for 27
    years, ever since Harry Truman was in the White House and you and I
    were learning how to get out of diapers. He's just doing his job. *(pause)*
    But what a rotten trick!
CHIEFIE: One of his range kids got hit, but it couldn't have been any of the
    long drive contestants because they just got down here. It probably was
    one of the touring pros who beaned his worker!

BIG CAT: The point is, I wouldn't mind any of this, you know, if only they had told us in advance. I would have planned my day different, you know that. I'm a nice guy, but I've got emotions. When something like this happens, it's hard for me to recover.

CHIEFIE: But Big Cat, we know all the other contestants have the same problem, right?

BIG CAT: True, but I'm the defending champion. They don't have nearly as much to lose as I do. Also, Chiefie, when I can practice with the other guys beforehand, I gain a certain psychological advantage. Because once they see me hit a few, they start to wonder what they're doing here.

CHIEFIE: People in official blazers, they're like my ex-boss at the warehouse, you know? Nazis.

BIG CAT: That's too extreme, but you're on the right track. Get in the car.

Scene 5: Valley Heights Golf Course, a public layout five miles from Oakmont and, in striking contrast to the championship site, totally devoid of activity right now except for a group of men clustered near the first tee who are wearing Bermuda shorts and biting down on dark cigars. It turns out they are waiting for the rest of their group to show up so they can tee off and get on with their weekly golf outing.

Big Cat explains his situation to the Valley Heights pro and obtains permission to drive a dozen balls back and forth on the nearest convenient fairways in an effort to prepare for the L.D.

Big Cat sprays his first batch of drives down the first fairway, then he and Chiefie, driving an electric cart, set off to retrieve them. The first tee slopes sharply and Chiefie, overly anxious to round up Big Cat's shots, nearly turns the cart over.

For the next half hour, Big Cat hits and Chiefie drives, Big Cat scooping up the balls as they go along. Big Cat is swinging with five or six different tempos, all of them fast. Chiefie finds himself at a rare loss for words. He concentrates on keeping the cart upright and prays that Big Cat will sort things out in his swing himself.

Finally, they return to the first tee where the men's group, now fully constituted, is ready to start their weekly tournament. Big Cat hits a half-dozen balls down the first fairway, none of them well. He invites the men to put the balls in their pocket if they come across them. Then, frustrated, he changes his target alignment completely. He hits his last three balls in the direction of a woods. He hits them as solidly as he has ever hit any ball, and they go straight and high and pure into the timber. The men gathered around are stupefied. All at once, Big Cat's chances look very good again to Chiefie.

The men give Big Cat a round of applause. They urge him to return later, after the contest, because they are going to tap two kegs and cook all the hamburgers a man can eat.

BIG CAT: *(on the way back to the car)* Chiefie, those are corner tavern folks. My kind of people.

Scene 6: Big Cat runs into a long line of traffic on the road back to Oakmont, with not enough time to sit it out. He decides to drive along the shoulder of the road on the right side, jockeying his Cougar between the cars stuck in the traffic and the bicyclists and dogs making their way alongside. He gains two miles and as much as 15 minutes this way, and cuts back into traffic a half mile short of the club. Then, when another delay appears ahead, he pulls his car out of traffic once more, this time across the southbound lane, and parks it in the nearest available space, which happens to be on the front lawn of a school.

Big Cat gets out of the car, opens the trunk, grabs his contest driver and heads back across the road in the direction of Oakmont's first tee, where L.D. IV is due to begin in 10 minutes.

BIG CAT: Get me something to drink, will you Chiefie?

Scene 7: The small grandstand that has been set up next to the first tee is packed. Hordes of other fans jostle each other for position on various knolls that seem to offer some vantage point. Still other fans are stretched out in lines four deep along both sides of the fairway all the way down to the target area, where yardage markers have been installed, a measuring team stands by, and a TV crew is poised on high in a cherry-picker.

Inside the ropes on the first tee, the 16 Long Drive finalists sit quietly on folding chairs in rows, looking for all their reputations as sluggers like the men's choir at the local village church. To one side is a long table manned by a dozen or so contest officials holding sharp pencils. On the other side, between two TV cameras, the ABC commentators for the event, Dave Marr and Dan Jenkins (of *Sports Illustrated* and *Semi-Tough* fame) sit wired up as though for the electric chair. Also in attendance are three dozen touring pros including Tom Watson, Tom Weiskopf and Ben Crenshaw.

Chiefie looks for an opening through which to bear the Coke that Big Cat has asked him to get. The crowd is dense and unyielding. Finally, he persuades a young female security guard to let him through the ropes on the far side of the tee. He makes his way alongside a precariously steep hill, sticks his head through a hedge and emerges near the seated contestants. Big Cat is located more to the other side of things, so Chiefie addresses Dave Marr at the nearby TV location.

CHIEFIE: Hey, Dave, would you pass this to Evan Williams?
DAVE MARR: *(taking off headset)* Ed who?
CHIEFIE: Evan—Big Cat!
DAVE MARR: *(taking Coke)* Sure!
CHIEFIE: Thanks!

At this point, Chiefie's loafers slide out from under him and he disappears through the hedge and down the hill. Dave Marr stares momentarily in disbelief, then passes Big Cat his Coke.

A smile from the first-round leader in the 1978 L.D. IV.

Scene 8: Round 1 of the Long Drive finals: the 16 contestants will each hit four balls; the six longest hitters will qualify for Round 2.

Chiefie paces behind the crowd as the contest begins. His cord suit has grass stains from his recent tumble. He looks as though he's just been let out on parole from somewhere. He catches glimpses of clubheads flashing at the top of backswings, but must rely on the announcements on the loud-speaker system following each contestant's efforts to know what is going on. He hears a lot of drives going under 300, and many others flying out of play, and he decides that Big Cat is in good shape for the competition in spite of his problems earlier.

By the time Big Cat hits, in the 11th position, Chiefie has located a spot from which he can enjoy a splendid view of the proceedings: the top of a fork-lift truck that happens to be parked in the area.

Big Cat's first ball goes 329 yards, 5 inches. There is a ringing round of applause. The drive puts him in the lead.

CHIEFIE: *(screaming)* Big Cat! I knew you could do it!!
MARSHAL: Hey you, get down from there!

No one hits it farther and at the end of the first round the standings are:

1. Evan Williams	329 yds.	5 inches
2. John McComish	328 yds.	8 inches
3. Victor Lahteine	324 yds.	24 inches
4. Cotton Dunn	319 yds.	27 inches
5. Ron Milanovich	312 yds.	7 inches
6. Billy Eastep	311 yds.	4 inches

Scene 9: Clubhouse bar.

CHIEFIE: Do you have any champagne for sale?
BARTENDER: Sure we got champagne.
CHIEFIE: Put one bottle on ice for me.
BARTENDER: What kind you want?
CHIEFIE: The one that's hardest to pronounce. That way I know it's quality.

Scene 10: First tee.

Round 2: The six remaining contestants will each hit three balls; the three longest hitters qualify for the third and final round. Yardages from the first round remain in force. In other words, to dethrone Big Cat, one of the five other contestants must hit the ball farther than 329 yards, 5 inches. A young amateur from Massachusetts does just that by a margin of 16 inches.

Chiefie, having discreetly climbed back up the fork-lift, hangs off the side of the thing with one hand and watches Big Cat, batting fourth this time, hit one ball out of play and the other two in the 300 yard range. What bothers Chiefie more than the fact that Big Cat has temporarily surrendered the lead is that Big Cat's three swings look quick and flat.

Leaders at the end of the second round:
1. Victor Lahteine   329 yds. 21 inches
2. Evan Williams   329 yds.   5 inches
3. John McComish   328 yds.   8 inches

Scene 11: Clubhouse bar.

BARTENDER: Ready for the champagne?
CHIEFIE: Not yet. What I need is a gin and tonic with hardly any tonic, you
    know what I mean?
BARTENDER: What about the champagne?
CHIEFIE: Hold off on that order for just a minute.

Scene 12: First tee.
Chiefie climbs back up the fork-lift truck with his gin and tonic.
Round 3 begins. The new leader hits first and fails to improve on his
lead.
    Big Cat stands up for his last three chances to remain the champ.
Chiefie swallows his gin and tonic whole.
    Big Cat hits his first ball out of play. He hits his second ball 310 yards.
He hits the third one 306.
    Chiefie climbs down from the fork-lift truck and walks slowly toward the
clubhouse.
    Meanwhile, the third contestant, another amateur, from Santa Maria,
California, connects on his second ball and hits it farther than Big Cat and the
first contestant.

Final results:
1. John McComish   330 yds. 19½ inches
2. Victor Lahteine   329 yds. 21   inches
3. Evan Williams   329 yds.   5   inches

Scene 13: Clubhouse bar.

BARTENDER: What'll it be?
CHIEFIE: Cancel the goddam champagne.

5 flying to another year

Time: Late Thursday morning, the day after L.D. IV. Cloudy skies.

Scene 1: Big Cat picks up Chiefie at his motel and they head for Oakmont. Big Cat does not appear unduly dejected about the misfortunes of yesterday. Morale-wise he bounced back quickly. After the contest, he spent several hours at Oakmont granting interviews and socializing with friends, then went out to a dinner party given by the L.D. sponsors. There he was his familiar amiable self, telling stories and even giving advice to John McComish, also in attendance, on how to hit the ball farther, and some ways to better his moves on the discotheque floor.

For Chiefie, the previous night was more problematic. Returning to his motel after the contest, he discovered that his beloved Triumph Bonneville had been stolen. He spent the better part of the evening describing the machine to the Monroeville Police Department.

In any event, as the two men drive out to Oakmont to watch some of the opening round of the PGA Championship, Big Cat is concerned not about his loss of the long drive title—which he figures to win back next year—but about his friend's loss of his motorcycle. And Chiefie is miserable, not because his Triumph is gone, but because his friend's triumph has not occurred.

Emotional wires thus crossed, they arrive at the course.

Scene 2: Arnold Palmer is leaning against a golf cart, under the trees next to the ninth green, signing autographs for a pack of kids. Big Cat and Chiefie wander by.

ARNIE: *(feigning indignation)* What happened out there yesterday, Big Cat? I put all my money on you!
BIG CAT: I did not get to hit my best shot, Arnold!
ARNIE: For crying out loud!
BIG CAT: What can I say!
ARNIE: Listen, you come visit me for a couple of days and we'll get your game ready for the tour.
BIG CAT: I'm willing!
ARNIE: I mean it. A little time together and I guarantee you'll be able to go out there and win it all. *(flashing the magical Arnold Palmer smile)* Course, I'll want my cut!
BIG CAT: Sure! *(after a pause)* Arnold, good luck to you out there this week, you know? *(as much to himself as to Chiefie, as they walk away)* That man is the King. He is still the King.

Scene 3: Dave Marr walks down the clubhouse steps and sees Big Cat.

MARR: What in the world went wrong out there, Short Knocker?
BIG CAT: *(shrugs)* Didn't get my shot! Never put my best swing on it!
MARR: That first ball you hit, I couldn't believe it went that far.
BIG CAT: I know! I hit it off the heel!
MARR: I couldn't believe it went 329.
BIG CAT: Anyway, I never got it together, Dave!
MARR: But you're still the longest hitting pro in the world, right? The other two guys were *amateurs.*
BIG CAT: So I still got a title!
MARR: Right! See you later!

Scene 4: Big Cat and Chiefie sit high in a grandstand watching some of the early foursomes play into the 18th green.

CHIEFIE: What if a good golfer were with you when you were warming up for the contest yesterday, instead of me? Another pro, say—he might have noticed something that could have helped you get it together.
BIG CAT: Maybe, but you still got to know your own swing.
CHIEFIE: I didn't help. I brought you bad luck.
BIG CAT: Naw, you were good company. Listen, there were a lot of things going wrong, when you stop to think about it. I mean, in addition to not being able to hit drivers off the practice tee here.
CHIEFIE: Like that Bible open to the "Book of Job!"
BIG CAT: Well, yeah, maybe. And a month ago they ran that feature on me in *S.I.* That's sometimes the kiss of death for an athlete who's been doing

125

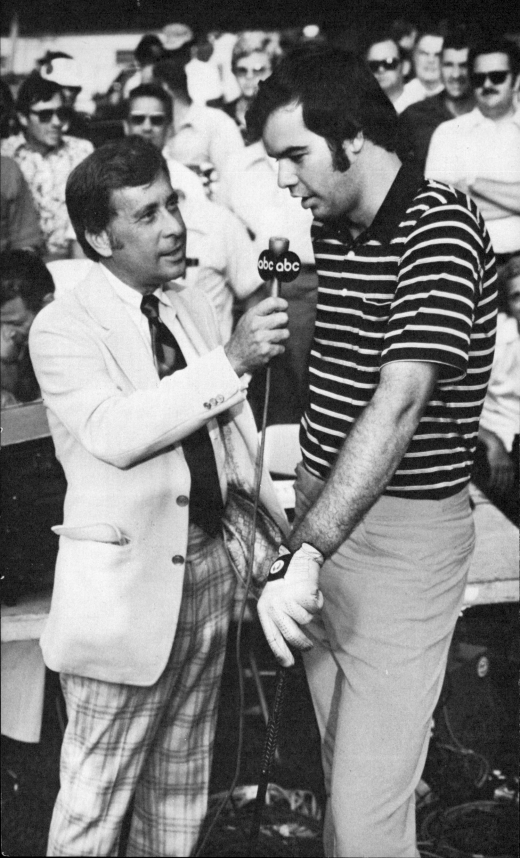

well. You finally get the publicity and then you go into a nosedive for some reason. Day before yesterday, they stop Pete Rose's hitting streak at 44 games, and that's no good either because I'm kind of on a streak, too, going for three in a row, you know? Then I hear on the radio that the comedian Totie Fields just died, who I met a couple of times, and that was too bad. It's crazy, I know, but these things coming together in time kind of suggest a pattern, good or bad, depending on what they are, and next thing you know, if you pay attention to them, you're part of the pattern.

Scene 5: An hour later. Big Cat is driving Chiefie to the airport. The moody skies finally open up and there is a downpour. Big Cat sets his wipers on Extra Fast.

BIG CAT: Scores are going to drop.
CHIEFIE: Why's that?
BIG CAT: The greens. They're going to hold better after all this rain. And they won't putt nearly as fast.
CHIEFIE: I hate to ask you this, Big Cat, but I didn't count on losing my bike. I'm a little short.
BIG CAT: I got cash, how much do you need?
CHIEFIE: Well, what does it cost to fly from Pittsburgh to Newark if you're not an eagle?

Scene 6: Inside terminal.
Awaiting Chiefie's flight out, Big Cat and Chiefie have a sandwich and check out newspaper coverage of the Long Driving Contest.

CHIEFIE: You still get most of the ink, even when you lose.
BIG CAT: *(grimly)* Yeah. *(looking up from newspaper)* You know, that's only the second long drive contest I've lost in my life?
CHIEFIE: Hey, will it hurt during the next year, losing?
BIG CAT: Maybe, maybe not. There's still nobody who can put on a long drive show the way I can. *(long pause)* But sure, it's possible I'll have more time between jobs from now on. *(After reflecting on what he has said, Big Cat's eyes light up.)* But look at the bright side.
CHIEFIE: What's that?
BIG CAT: If the year goes by more slowly, it means I live longer!
CHIEFIE: I never thought of that!
BIG CAT: *(hearing announcement on P.A. system)* There's your flight now, Chiefie. C'mon, I'll walk you to the gate. . . .

**Dave Marr interviews
    Big Cat after he
      narrowly loses.**